MENTAL FITNESS

Your Scientific Blueprint
To Health, Power and Purpose
From A Real Medical Doctor
(Not Another Wannabe Guru Book)

By Adam Rajoulh, MD

Copyright © 2025 by Adam Rajoulh, MD

All rights reserved. No part of this book may be reproduced or transmitted in any form or by any means, electronic or mechanical, including photocopying, recording, or by any information storage and retrieval system, without written permission from the author, except in the case of brief quotations in reviews or critical articles.

Printed in the United States of America

ISBN: 979-8-9937915-1-7

Dedication

I dedicate this book to my parents, for all their sacrifices and their continuous love, support, and faith in me.

To my beautiful daughter Leena, my greatest blessing, for giving me a purpose bigger than myself and for teaching me the true meaning of unconditional love.

To God, for allowing me the opportunity to help others live healthier, more powerful, and more purposeful lives.

And finally, to anyone who has the courage to face failure, rise again, and keep moving forward, this book is for you.

Letter From The Author

This is not another sugarcoated wannabe guru book. Just real strategies, stories, and science to help you unlock health, power, and purpose.

You already have what it takes. You don't need another influencer telling you to wake up at 4 a.m. and drink celery juice. What you need is clarity, mental toughness, and practical tools that you can actually use and implement every single day. Read it. Highlight it. Go back to it. The "Power Protocol" is your roadmap to greatness.

I didn't write this to impress you. I wrote this to impact you. Whether it's your health, your finances, your mindset, or your purpose, there is something in these pages that will make you stronger. The mission is simple: to help you cut through the noise, reclaim control, and build a stronger mind, body, and spirit.

So here's my promise: if you actually apply what's in these chapters, you will walk away with at least one thing, a tool, a perspective, a spark, that will improve your life. You'll think differently. You'll move differently. You'll live differently.

Life is your biggest blessing. And wasting it is the biggest tragedy. Let's get started.

Table of Contents

Chapter 1 - Mental Fitness   1
Building Strength of Mind as the Foundation of Everything

Chapter 2 - Not Another Wannabe Guru   13
Cutting Through Fake Experts and Empty Motivation

Chapter 3 - You Have Already Won   23
Gratitude, Perspective, and Starting From a Place of Blessing

Chapter 4 - Fitness Saved My Life   31
How Training Gave Me Confidence, Discipline, and Purpose

Chapter 5 - Nutrition And Gut Health   41
Fueling the Body and Mind; Evidence Based Diet Principles

Chapter 6 - Kill Stress Before It Kills You   53
Tactics and Science Backed Methods to Master Stress

Chapter 7 - Don't Sleep On Sleep   59
Optimizing Recovery, Sleep Cycles, and Longevity

Chapter 8 - The Power Protocol   67
My Daily Blueprint – 5 Pillars: Gratitude, Training, Nutrition, Sleep, Mindset

Chapter 9 - Failure And Resilience   77
Owning Hardship, Rejecting the Victim Mentality, and Pivoting Through Adversity

Chapter 10 - Money Moves - Financial Fitness 85
Financial Discipline, Investing, and Creating a Legacy of Stability

Chapter 11 - Digital Discipline: Rewiring Your Brain In The Age Of Distraction 95
Attention, Dopamine, and Building Mental Fitness in the Digital Age

Chapter 12 - Respect And Healthy Relationships 101
Building Bonds, Trust, and Surrounding Yourself With the Right People

Chapter 13 - Serving Others - A Legacy Of Purpose 111
Why True Success Means Giving Back and Leaving Impact

Mental Fitness 30 Day Challenge 117
Practical Steps to Put This Book Into Action, Every Single Day

References 125

About The Author 137

Chapter 1

Mental Fitness

"The mind is everything. What you think you become."

— Buddha

Your mind is the strongest muscle you'll ever train. And like every muscle, it only grows when you push it past comfort into pain. Most people lose the fight before the day even starts; they wake up already defeated, replaying yesterday's mistakes like a shitty mixtape.

Mental fitness means cutting that loop off at the source. It means mastering your thoughts instead of letting them master you. It means separating what you can control from what you can't and then having the courage to push your mind into discomfort the way you push your body under a heavy barbell.

Here's the truth: your thoughts are either chains or jet fuel. They'll either drag you down or launch you forward. And every day, you get to decide which.

Mental Fitness: The Foundation of Everything

This really is everything. *Mental fitness* isn't a "bonus" to the real work. It is the real work. You can have the perfect workout plan, the cleanest diet, and a supportive circle, but if your mindset isn't trained, none of it sticks.

I call it *fitness* because that's exactly what it is: a discipline, a lifestyle, a muscle. Just like your body, your mind grows stronger only when you stress it, recover, and repeat.

Just like physical fitness strengthens your muscles, *mental fitness* strengthens your ability to handle stress, control your thoughts, and stay focused under pressure.

At its core, mental fitness is:

- **Emotional resilience** – bouncing back after setbacks instead of staying stuck.
- **Cognitive discipline** – training your thoughts so they work for you, not against you.
- **Focus and clarity** – filtering out distractions and staying aligned with your goals.
- **Stress management** – keeping calm under pressure instead of breaking.
- **Positive perspective** – intentionally directing your mind toward gratitude and solutions instead of negativity and problems.

Master Your Mind

Mastery of the inner world precedes mastery of the outer world. In *The Master Key System* (Charles F. Haanel, 1912), the central lesson is that thought shapes reality. Focused, disciplined thinking creates strength and success, while scattered or negative thinking leads to weakness and defeat. Haanel taught that concentration, visualization, and persistence are the tools to direct the mind's energy toward a clear vision.

Mental fitness is about training your attention like a muscle by guarding it against distraction, holding it steady through adversity, and refusing to let circumstances dictate your purpose. Strength begins within.

The Power of the Subconscious

The subconscious mind shapes habits, creativity, and intuition long before we rationalize them. Carl Jung called it the hidden architect of behavior, and neuroscience shows decisions often start subconsciously before awareness even kicks in (Soon et al., 2008).

In mental fitness, this is where discipline becomes transformation: through meditation, visualization, and flow, you train your subconscious to embed the right patterns. You absorb positivity and creativity and deflect negativity and destruction.

Learning the rewarding practice of turning off your conscious thoughts and tapping into your subconscious is a form of self- awareness and superpower that money can't buy.

Choosing What Matters

Most people drain their energy by worrying about everything, seeking approval, avoiding discomfort, or obsessing over problems that don't matter in the long run. Real strength comes from narrowing your focus to what truly counts. *Mental fitness* isn't about eliminating struggle; it's about choosing struggles that align with your values and purpose.

Mental fitness means recognizing that problems never disappear, they only get replaced. Growth comes when you pick the problems worth having, accept responsibility, and stop chasing happiness as if it were a destination.

And let's not forget about the haters. Anyone doing better than you doesn't have time to hate. They're too busy building. Haters only come from below. Nobody above you is throwing stones. Those above you don't hate. They inspire.

Real freedom is found in saying "no" more often: no to distractions, no to empty validation, and no to living someone else's definition of success. The less attention you waste on what doesn't matter, the more power you have to invest in what truly does. Not every battle is worth your cortisol.

Believe in Yourself

Believing in yourself is both the first and last step in any journey of growth. Remember, your life is controlled by your perception of yourself. Without that inner conviction, no strategy, no program, and no coach can move you forward.

When you've reached the finish line, whether it's recovering your health, hitting a career milestone, or transforming your mindset, the victory still comes back to belief. Half the battle is won the moment you decide that you are capable. The other half is sustained by returning to that same belief when things get tough. In this way, success begins with faith in yourself and ends with faith in yourself.

Taking Ownership

You cannot have power without taking complete responsibility for your life, your failures, weaknesses, environment, and choices. When you keep blaming others, you are simply giving away your power.

It all starts with shifting your mindset. Instead of "Why me?" ask "What can I do?" This flips victimhood into action. Taking ownership is the foundation for growth and power because it keeps the steering wheel in your hands.

Mental fitness is not about being happy all the time or avoiding struggle. It's about building the inner strength to face challenges head-on, control what you can, and refuse to quit when life gets heavy.

Comfort Zones or Coffins

From childhood, we have been "domesticated" by society. We have been conditioned to follow rules, beliefs, and expectations imposed by parents, schools, and culture. While some of these rules and norms are necessary, some may be self-limiting. Comfort zones sound nice, but they're just coffins with better lighting. Stay there long enough and your dreams rot.

Pain is the spark that shatters comfort. Don't mistake pain or failure for the end, it's the beginning. It's the door you kick open to transcend into something greater. If you feel pain, congratulations, you're alive. You're moving and you're on the edge of growth.

If I hadn't broken my comfort zone, I never would've written this book. Pivoting, evolving, adapting, that's the human program. Stay stagnant and you're basically choosing slow death over growth.

The Three Desires That Drive Us

Strip everything down and humans chase three desires: *wealth, health, and love.*

- **Wealth.** Not because money buys happiness (it doesn't), but because poverty guarantees misery. Try being your best self when you can't pay rent. Wealth isn't everything, but without it, life is survival, not living.
- **Health.** If you lose this, none of the other desires matter. Ask any patient in a hospital bed and you will see most would trade everything to feel normal again.
- **Love.** Humans weren't built for isolation. We need to give and receive love. That connection is what separates us from animals.

Neglect any one of these, and the other two collapse. But if you want to keep them all alive, you need one thing first: *Mental Fitness.* Without it, wealth corrupts you, love betrays you, and health slips away.

The Science of Mental Fitness

Mental fitness isn't just philosophy, it's physiology. Research on neuroplasticity shows the brain literally rewires itself in response to thought and habit (Pascual-Leone et al., 2005). That means your mental patterns carve grooves into your biology. Gratitude, visualization, and positive self-talk done repeatedly don't just "make you feel good." They physically reshape your brain.

Think of neuroplasticity like a plastic bag: it stretches, it reshapes, it adapts. But leave garbage in it long enough, and it stinks. Same with your thoughts.

Daily gratitude, physical training, meditation, and prayer aren't just motivational slogans. They're neurological hacks. They pump dopamine, serotonin, and endorphins into your system. They train your brain to recognize opportunity instead of doom.

This is why monks can sit in silence while the world burns, and Navy SEALs can stay calm while chaos explodes around them. Their brains aren't magic; they're trained.

The Law of Attraction: You Get What You Focus

The "Law of Attraction" gets tossed around like some cosmic vending machine. "Think happy thoughts and the universe spits out Lamborghinis and supermodels." Sorry, it doesn't work like that.

The Law of Attraction is simple physics. Your mind is a magnet. Whatever you focus on expands. If you obsess over problems, you'll see more problems. If you lock in on solutions, opportunities will start showing up everywhere. In short: *what you focus on, you pull toward you.*

But here's the part the self-help gurus won't tell you: attraction without action is masturbation. Visualization is step one. Work is step two. Manifestation is step three. If you skip the middle part, the sweat, the grind, the discipline, you're just daydreaming.

Want love? Be loving. Want respect? Start by respecting yourself. Want wealth? Create value, not excuses. Your life mirrors your mindset, for better or worse.

The Law of Attraction in plain English:
- Think like a loser → act like a loser → lose.
- Think like a winner → act like a winner → fight like hell → eventually win.

That's it. No crystals required.

The Law of Abundance: Stop Thinking Small

Abundance is the antidote to scarcity. Scarcity says life is a pie, if someone else takes a slice, you're left with crumbs. Abundance says the oven is always on and you can bake your own damn pie.

Living in abundance doesn't mean cash rains down on you. It means training your brain to see opportunity instead of obstacles. Scarcity makes you hoard, envy, and fear. Abundance makes you create, build, and give.

Science backs it up: an abundance mindset increases resilience, creativity, and collaboration. Fear shuts your brain down. Abundance switches it on.

- Scarcity says: *"If they win, I lose."*
- Abundance says: *"If they win, that means winning is possible for me too."*
- Scarcity says: *"Resources are limited."*
- Abundance says: *"I'll find a way to create more."*

Here's the bottom line: Abundance isn't about waiting for blessings.

It's realizing you're already standing in the middle of one.

Habit Formation

Psychologists like Charles Duhigg and James Clear popularized the idea of the habit loop: *cue → routine → reward.*

- Cue: the trigger (morning alarm).
- Routine: the behavior (put on gym shoes).
- Reward: the feeling (endorphin rush, self respect).

By hacking the cue and the reward, you can rewire the routine. Pairing a new habit with an existing one, called *habit stacking*, is one of the fastest ways to build discipline.

Example: *"After I brush my teeth, I'll write three things I'm grateful for."*

Fail Forward: The Power of Rejection

Every success story hides a graveyard of failures.

Howard Schultz (CEO of Starbucks) was turned down by over **200 banks** before anyone would fund his coffee shop vision.

J.K. Rowling was rejected by **12 publishers** before Harry Potter saw daylight.

Albert Einstein didn't speak fluently until age four, and one of his teachers told him he would "never amount to much."

These weren't anomalies. They were patterns. Greatness is never a clean sprint; it's a bloody marathon of rejection, self-doubt, and persistence.

So next time you fail, don't whine about the closed door. That rejection is a rep. Do enough reps, and strength follows.

Perspective Is Key

Mental fitness is perspective. You can either fixate on what's missing, or you can focus on what's present.

Lose a job? You didn't lose your hands, your brain, or your ability to try again.

Fail in love? You didn't lose your capacity to give or to receive it.

Screw up royally? Good. Now you've got a scar that proves you were in the fight.

Perspective turns stress into training. Gratitude turns losses into lessons. And together, they build the strongest kind of wealth, the kind no recession, no betrayal, and no illness can take.

Why This Book Exists

I'm not writing this because it sounds good. I'm writing this because I've lived it.

Nobody is paying me to write this book, and I'm not paying anyone else to ghostwrite it. I've been writing this book for **39 years.** Not with a pen, but with my life. Every scar, every failure, every lesson has been inked onto these pages long before I typed a single word.

As a physician, I've seen patients with the odds stacked against them who still fought and won. I've also seen others with every advantage throw it away because they quit mentally before their body quit physically.

As a father, I've learned that your kids don't need half of you, they need all of you. That only happens when your mind is trained.

And as a man who has failed more times than he can count, I've learned this: you don't rise because life got easier. You rise because you got stronger.

This book is the blueprint to **health, power, and purpose.** But whether you use it or not, that's on you.

Win or lose,
the choice is yours.

"Your life is dictated by your thoughts."

— Adam Rajoulh, MD

Chapter 2

Not Another Wannabe Guru

"Beware of false prophets, who come to you in sheep's clothing but inwardly are ravenous wolves."

— Matthew 7:15

The Guru Problem

Scroll through Amazon or social media or step into a bookstore, and you're buried under a tidal wave of "self-help experts." Motivational speakers with no credentials. "Fitness influencers" whose physiques owe more to Photoshop, peptides, or pharmacy grade testosterone than to discipline. Life coaches who've never actually lived. And then there's the endless parade of funnel selling hustlers: recycled motivational fluff designed to siphon your wallet faster than it improves your life.

That's not me.

This book isn't another pep rally for the attention-deficient, nor is it a Pinterest board of half-baked affirmations. It's not "pseudoscience meets hustle culture" or "say it, manifest it, and your dream body will appear." That stuff sells tickets, not results.

Red Flags of a Fake Guru:
- No qualifications, credentials are vague or meaningless ("certified life architect, mentor, or life coach" mean nothing without any real credentials)
- Never cite peer-reviewed research or real clinical data.
- "Before and after" photos look suspiciously edited.
- Sell shortcuts: "Six-pack abs in 7 days!"
- Push more supplements than actual strategies.
- Use fear or shame to sell ("If you don't buy my course, you'll fail forever").
- Dodge hard questions with motivational fluff.

Green Flags of a Real Expert:
- They have real credentials and qualifications to make claims
- Reference real science (journals, clinical studies, established practice).
- Admit limitations: no one has all the answers.
- Focus on long term discipline and results over hacks.
- Their success is reproducible: students, patients, or clients also see results.
- Practice what they preach (their lifestyle matches their message).
- Their advice holds up even when you strip away the sales funnel.

Why Listen to Me

I'm a board-certified hospitalist physician and a trusted medical voice with more than a decade of frontline experience.

Supported by over 100 references drawn from clinical research, psychology, and philosophy, *Mental Fitness* is not just a matter of opinion but a scientific blueprint that you can trust. As a fellow scientist, I know firsthand that data is king.

I treat all types of disease from heart attacks and strokes to life-threatening infections. I've seen the price people pay for neglecting their health. I've also seen the incredible transformations when discipline, resilience, and lifestyle changes pull someone back from the edge.

This unique perspective gives me both authority and responsibility. I'm not here to keep you alive on machines, I want you to live, *powerfully.*

My Path Here

I didn't take the straight path. I started as a psychology major, fascinated by how thoughts shape behavior and how much the mind dictates reality. My original plan was psychiatry. But when I rotated through hospitals, I saw something raw and undeniable: the unfiltered frontlines of human health.

I pivoted into hospital medicine, where I could merge my background in psychology with the urgency of saving lives. That duality, the mind and the body, science and grit, still drives me.

Death and Regret

Part of my job means facing life and death on a regular basis. I've run countless CPR codes, I've saved lives, and I've also lost patients despite every effort. In those moments, you develop a deeper gratitude and humility for the fragility of life itself. I've been present for many final breaths, especially during the COVID pandemic, and what strikes me as profoundly tragic is not just the loss of life, but the regret that often lingers in those final moments.

Seeing patients die with regret has taught me a lesson that I carry with me: tomorrow is never guaranteed. So ask yourself now: what's my why? Why am I here? What is my true purpose?

Because the greatest loss is not death itself, but living without ever having truly lived and dying with regret.

No Hacks. No Hormones. No Bullshit.

Let me be clear: I'm all natural. I've never abused steroids, testosterone, or peptides. No shortcuts, no hacks, no smoke-and-mirror trickery. Everything I teach comes from lived experience and evidence based medicine.

I don't believe in hacks. The word itself has been hijacked. "Life hack" implies you can shortcut your way to something worth having. But there are no shortcuts to character, no secret codes to resilience.

Research shows habit formation takes, on average, 66 days of consistent effort (Lally et al., *European Journal of Social Psychology*, 2009). Not 7 days. Not 30. Sixty-six. That's not a hack. That's discipline.

If someone tries to sell you a shortcut, ask yourself: *Would I want this on my obituary?* "Here lies Dave, he hacked his way to greatness." I didn't think so.

I'm Not Perfect and Neither Are You

I don't have all the answers, and I never will. Nobody does. I'm not here to posture as perfect, I'm far from it. I've been through failure, heartbreak, financial collapse, and loss. The difference? I refuse to let those moments define me.

And let's be clear: perfection is a myth. Humans are born imperfect, and that's not a flaw, it's our design. What separates us from angels or machines is free will, the ability to make choices, screw up, learn, and adapt. We are wired to sin, stumble, and get back up again.

Perfection isn't just unattainable; it runs against the very grain of human nature and evolution. Evolution itself is the story of trial, error, and adaptation. If life were perfect, there would be no growth. No progress. No evolution.

Improvement, on the other hand, is real, but it's not a final destination. It's not a mountaintop you plant your flag on. It's a process, a daily practice. Every rep in the gym, every disciplined choice in your diet, every hard conversation you don't avoid, that's improvement. And the beauty of it is that there's no finish line.

That's why chasing perfection will leave you burned out and bitter, but embracing imperfection will leave you stronger, wiser, and more resilient than you ever thought possible.

My Daughter Gave Me Superpowers

Power has destroyed kings, corrupted prophets, and poisoned entire nations. But here's the truth: before my daughter was born, I was powerless. Powerless to my own demons. Powerless to my own flaws. Powerless to myself.

Then she arrived. And in that moment, my entire existence shifted. She became the realest thing in my life. Everything was about her. My purpose, my legacy, my very survival became tied to those small, innocent eyes looking up at me. Eyes that depend on me. Eyes that I refuse to let down.

The day I delivered my daughter in the hospital with my own hands, I gained a new kind of power, a superpower I didn't even know existed. The kind of power that makes you hungrier, sharper, more disciplined. Because when another life depends on you, there's no room for excuses.

I would give my life for my daughter. I would go to war with the world for her. And in that relentless, uncompromising love, I have found the greatest strength of my life. I am no longer living for myself. I am living for an extension of myself, the better extension. The innocent extension. My daughter. My angel. My Leena.

And no, you don't need to have a child to gain this kind of power. You don't have to be a parent to feel this. But you do need a purpose bigger than yourself, a person, a mission, a cause. Without it, you wander. With it, you transcend.

The Patient Who Believed the Wrong Gurus

I once treated a man in his early 50s who collapsed at work. He had diabetes, high blood pressure, and heart failure. He'd been ignoring his health for years. But here's the kicker: he wasn't ignoring *everything*. He was spending hundreds of dollars a month on "miracle" supplements he found online, recommended by a slick influencer who promised energy, fat-burning, and vitality.

When I told him he'd need surgery and lifelong medication, he broke down and said, *"Doc, I thought I was doing the right thing. I really believed those pills were helping me."*

That moment hit me hard. He wasn't lazy, and he wasn't stupid. He was misled. Sold a dream by a false prophet in gym shorts with a ring light.

That's why I'm writing this book. Because the wrong guidance doesn't just cost people money, it costs them their health, their dignity, and sometimes their life.

Why We Still Feel Stuck

Here's the paradox: even if you're not falling for snake-oil supplements, most of us are still stuck. Stress, toxic habits, broken relationships, ultra-processed food, endless scrolling, sleepless nights. We sabotage ourselves daily. Science backs this up:

- **Sleep deprivation** raises the risk of depression, obesity, and heart disease (CDC, 2016).
- **Chronic stress** rewires the brain, shrinking areas tied to memory and self-control (McEwen, *Nat Neurosci*, 2007).
- **Ultra-processed diets** increase rates of anxiety and depression (*JAMA Psychiatry*, 2023).

And yet we shrug, scroll, snack, and repeat. We trade eight hours of sleep for eight hours of comparing ourselves to strangers on Instagram. Then we wonder why we feel like garbage.

Mental Fitness: **The Missing Link**

Somewhere along the way, we lost the one thing that drives everything else: mental fitness.

Motivation fades. Inspiration dies by Monday morning. But mental fitness, the discipline of training your mind like you would train a muscle, that sticks. That compounds.

Studies on **resilience** show that people who practice deliberate cognitive strategies, reframing negative events, controlling daily habits, focusing on process not outcome, are far more likely to thrive after trauma (Tedeschi & Calhoun, 2004). This isn't speculation. It's science.

Not a Guru. A Blueprint.

I'm not your guru. I'm not here to sell you magic pills or whisper sweet affirmations. I'm a doctor who has faced failure, pain, and rock bottom, and clawed my way back. I'm a father who found purpose beyond himself. I'm a man who has stood face-to-face with death and knows that every single breath is an opportunity to build strength, discipline, and purpose.

This book isn't about me telling you what to think. It's about handing you a **blueprint,** *The Power Protocol*: a system that combines science, raw experience, and gritty tools. Something you can actually implement to build a healthier, stronger, more purposeful life.

Later in this book in *Chapter 8,* I'll show you exactly how I structure my days in my "Power Protocol." Gratitude. Training. Diet. Sleep. Mindset. Five pillars. No fluff, no hacks, no guru promises, just the same daily system I live by and teach. But before we get there, we need to build the foundation.

"I'm not here to be your guru. I'm here to strip away the lies, show you what works, and hand you the tools. The rest is on you."

— Adam Rajoulh, MD

Chapter 3

You Have Already Won

"It is not happiness that makes us grateful, it is gratefulness that makes us happy."

— Brother David Steindl-Rast

Against All Odds

The fact that you're here is already a statistical miracle. The odds of you being alive, with your exact DNA, reading this book, are about **1 in 400 trillion**. Out of every possible genetic roll of the dice, every war your ancestors survived, every random accident avoided, you made it.

You have a pulse. You can think. You can choose. That alone means you've already won the biggest lottery there is.

Life Is Your Biggest Blessing

When you wake up in the morning and lift yourself out of bed in a heated home, that's a blessing.

When you turn on the shower and have clean, running water, that's a blessing.

When you brush your teeth, walk downstairs, and open a fridge full of food, that's a blessing.

When you can get into a car and drive yourself to work, while complaining about traffic and your annoying job, yes, still a blessing.

We take these things for granted every day, myself included. But sometimes I remind myself: I'm alive. I'm here. And that is the greatest blessing of all.

Don't waste it. Don't take your health, your time, or your gifts for granted. Every day you get to wake up is another chance to become the best version of yourself.

Perspective Changes Everything

Here's the truth: whenever something goes bad for me, I always remind myself, it could be worse.

Bad day at work? Turn on the news and watch what's happening in the Middle East. Picky child who doesn't want to eat her vegetables? I showed my daughter a video of a homeless, hungry child. She's six, but she's smart enough to get it, I only had to show her once.

As a physician, perspective hits me in the gut every single day. Anytime I feel sorry for myself, I think of a young, healthy patient who died from a rare condition. Or a pediatric patient diagnosed with cancer. Whatever hardship you're carrying, someone out there would pray to have your "problems."

Perspective doesn't erase pain, but it makes gratitude possible.

The Science of Gratitude

Gratitude isn't just a Hallmark-card slogan. It's neuroscience.

Studies show that practicing gratitude:

- Lowers stress and anxiety (Emmons & McCullough, 2003).
- Strengthens the immune system (Sansone & Sansone, 2010).
- Improves sleep quality (Wood et al., 2009).
- Enhances relationships (Algoe, 2012).
- Increases overall life satisfaction and longevity.

Here's why: gratitude increases **dopamine** and **serotonin**, your brain's "happy hormones." They're the same chemicals that light up when you eat dessert or have sex. In other words, gratitude is nature's antidepressant, and it's free.

Over time, gratitude literally rewires the brain to look for positives instead of negatives. That's not fluff. That's fMRI data.

Gratitude and fMRI

Functional Magnetic Resonance Imaging (fMRI) lets scientists see how different brain regions "light up" in response to experiences. Think of it like watching the brain's electrical circuits flicker on a live screen while someone feels gratitude, stress, or joy.

What fMRI studies show about gratitude:

- Gratitude activates the medial prefrontal cortex: the same region tied to decision making and emotional regulation (Kini et al., *Front Psychol*, 2016).

- People who regularly practice gratitude show greater connectivity between the amygdala and prefrontal cortex, which means better control of fear and stress responses (Fox et al., *Soc Cogn Affect Neurosci*, 2015).

Translation: Gratitude literally rewires the brain so you default less to anxiety and more to resilience.

Gratitude and Immunity

Gratitude doesn't just change your mindset; it strengthens your body's defenses. When you practice gratitude, stress hormones like cortisol drop, while protective processes in the immune system become more active. In a study of patients with heart failure, those who kept gratitude journals showed lower inflammation markers like C-reactive protein and better heart rate variability, signs of a stronger, more resilient body (Mills et al., 2015).

Other research found gratitude practices can raise levels of immunoglobulin A (IgA), an antibody that helps fight infections in the respiratory tract (McCraty et al., 1998). In plain English: gratitude literally primes your immune system to fight back harder. It's free medicine, as powerful for your health as it is for your mood.

Bottom line, being thankful won't just warm your heart, it might even keep you from catching the next cold. Gratitude is like handing your immune system brass knuckles.

Gratitude vs. Entitlement

We live in a society drowning in stress, comparison, and dissatisfaction.

Social media sells us curated highlight reels of people who look richer, fitter, happier with rented lambos who can't even pay their rent. News cycles feed us chaos and disaster 24/7. No wonder people feel like they're constantly falling behind.

But gratitude isn't about ignoring problems. It's about confronting life with clarity. It's saying: *I may not have everything I want, but I have more than enough to keep moving forward.*

Gratitude is the antidote to entitlement. Without it, stress feels overwhelming. With it, even the worst days are reframed.

Practical Ways to Build Gratitude

- **Keep a gratitude journal.**

    Write down three things you're thankful for daily.

- **Say it out loud.**

    Don't wait until someone's gone to tell them you appreciate them.

    Use perspective triggers. Complaining about slow Wi-Fi? Imagine being in a hospital bed hooked up to a ventilator. Suddenly, lag doesn't matter.

- **Replace comparison with compassion.**

    When jealousy hits, flip it. If someone else can achieve it, so can you.

- **Start your day with thankfulness.** Start and end your day with gratitude, it's a better habit loop than doom-scrolling.
- **Volunteering and Service**

Volunteering at a hospital or soup kitchen will give you perspective that people have it much worse than you and will also allow you the opportunity to help those in need.

And if you want a life hack: the next time you're whining about how Starbucks ran out of oat milk, remember, there's a kid somewhere right now who would give anything just to have *milk*. Perspective is undefeated.

The Power of Mother Nature

Gratitude isn't only about journaling blessings; it's about noticing the gifts already around you. One of the most overlooked sources of healing is right outside your door: nature. Research shows that being in natural environments reduces cortisol, lowers blood pressure, and restores focus (Park et al., 2010; Bratman et al., 2015). The Japanese practice of *shinrin-yoku* ("forest bathing") has even been shown to boost immune function and increase your body's natural defense cells (Li et al., 2008).

Beyond biology, there's the spiritual reset. Standing at the ocean, walking a forest trail, or even sitting in your backyard reminds you that life is bigger than your stress. Gratitude becomes effortless when you're surrounded by God's creation. And while nature reminds us of creation all around us, prayer reminds us of the Creator within reach.

The Power of Prayer

Gratitude often starts with noticing blessings, but prayer takes it one step further, it turns gratitude into connection. Prayer is more than a religious act; it's both a form of mindfulness and a resilience anchor. Studies show that prayer is linked to lower anxiety, stronger emotional regulation, and better overall health (Anderson & Nunnelley, 2019). In other words, prayer isn't just a matter of faith, it's a scientifically supported tool for well-being.

Unlike venting or distraction, prayer doesn't deplete you, it restores you. It gives perspective when life feels overwhelming and helps you anchor yourself to something greater than the problem in front of you. Think of it as the original wireless connection, always available, no passcode required. Whether whispered in silence or spoken aloud, prayer is a practice that deepens gratitude, reduces stress, and strengthens purpose.

Gratitude as Resilience

Gratitude doesn't make life easier.

It makes you stronger.

It doesn't erase hardship, but it gives you the fuel to endure it. The patient who counts blessings fights harder than the one who wallows in "why me." The parent who models gratitude raises a child who's tougher, sharper, and more compassionate.

Reflection Exercise

Tonight, grab a notebook and answer:
1. What 3 things am I grateful for today, no matter how small?
2. What hardship am I facing that could be a hidden blessing?
3. Who in my life deserves to hear my gratitude before it's too late?

(Do this daily for 30 days. Your brain will thank you with stronger wiring.)

Remember, *Gratitude is not weakness. It's a weapon.*

> *"If you woke up today, you already won. Life itself is your biggest blessing."*

— Adam Rajoulh, MD

Chapter 4

Fitness Saved My Life

"I hated every minute of training, but I said, 'Don't quit. Suffer now and live the rest of your life as a champion.'"

— Muhammad Ali

From Weakness to Strength

When I started my freshman year of high school, I weighed 102 pounds and couldn't even bench press the bar (45 pounds). I was ridiculed. I was bullied. People saw me as weak and truthfully, I felt weak.

That summer, I decided to rewrite my story. While my friends were out enjoying themselves, I locked myself in the basement with the weights. They hardly saw me all summer. When I came back, I wasn't the same kid. I had gained nearly 20 pounds of muscle. I was stronger. I was faster. And most importantly, I was more confident.

That decision to grind when no one was watching changed my life. It taught me that transformation is possible if you're willing to show up every day and put in the work.

Training: My Sanctuary

I don't go to the gym because I have to. I go to the gym because I need to.

Training keeps me sharp, focused, and lethal. The gym provides a sanctuary where I can converse, face, and cripple my demons. While I can do this at any time, it starts in the gym.

Fitness isn't optional. It isn't vanity. It isn't about flexing in the mirror or posting a photo online. Fitness is my outlet, my therapy, my medicine.

No Tripods. No Texts. Just War.

The gym isn't my photo studio. It's my battlefield.

No tripods. No selfies. No endless scrolling.

While they pose and text, I punish and torment my demons.

My sanctuary is sweat.

My therapy is pain.

Every rep is war.

Every set is suffering.

I abuse my body to remind myself: pain is necessary.

Nobody here worked harder than ME.

Pain is strength. Pain is progress.

If you leave the gym comfortable without limping and dripping sweat, you never show up. Do work!

My (Power) Routine

As I'll talk about in Chapter 5 (Nutrition and Gut Health), the same way there's no perfect diet, there's also no perfect workout. Everyone's looking for the next secret, the miracle diet, the new workout trend, the magic pill, even the latest Ozempic. **But there is no magic.**

Just like your nutrition, your training will be built on one thing:

consistency.

At nearly 40, I've had to adapt. I can't train the way I did in my 20s. That doesn't mean training less, it means training smarter.

And because I'm also a father and a physician, I don't always have unlimited time. If I get to the gym four or five days a week, I consider that a win. On the days I can't, I train at home, whether it's running, bag work, or bodyweight workouts in the sun, I keep my body moving seven days a week.

Movement is key. Study after study shows that consistent physical activity significantly reduces all-cause mortality, regardless of age.[1]

I perform heavy compound movements first (squats, deadlifts, presses) followed by varied lighter accessory work after. I don't follow a "perfect" routine. What I do have is a consistent plan of attack:

Example of a Weekly Split (Repeat cycle through the week)
- **Monday:** Chest, triceps, legs
- **Tuesday:** Shoulders, back, legs
- **Wednesday:** Biceps, legs
- **Thursday:** Chest, triceps, legs
- **Friday:** Shoulders, back, legs
- **Saturday:** Biceps, legs

When I train a muscle, I hit it from every angle. If it's chest, that means bench press, incline, decline, dumbbells, cables, as many variations as possible. I don't always repeat the same workout, but I always have a game plan for which muscles I'm targeting and for how long.

After or before weight resistance training, I include at least 20–30 minutes of sauna. It isn't just recovery for me, it's therapy. It's where I sweat out stress, clear my head, and reset my soul. Fitness is so ingrained in me now that it's not something I "find time for." It's something I live by.

And here's the truth: **when I leave the gym, I make sure I'm dripping in sweat.** If you're just starting out, that's your only non- negotiable, leave the gym sweating. Veterans or beginners, the principle is the same: sweat is the proof of purpose.

For those who can't train traditionally, like my older patients with arthritis or joint problems, I recommend swimming. It's not about matching someone else's program. It's about consistent, purposeful movement that keeps your body alive and your spirit sharp.

Training is about more than strength. It's about adapting, pivoting, and respecting recovery as much as intensity. It's not just about working out hard; it's about working out smart.

Confidence, Discipline, and Purpose

Bodybuilding and training didn't just build muscle; they built me. They gave me confidence, discipline, and purpose. These are three traits that are non-negotiable if you want to succeed in anything worth a damn.

Bodybuilding started as a means of survival, but it became the highlight of my day. It has helped mold me into the man and the father that I am today. It taught me how to set goals and pursue them relentlessly. It gave me the mindset that I can achieve anything I put my mind to. It transformed me into something more: stronger, sharper, and harder to break.

The weights didn't just sculpt my body; they forged my character. They burned away excuses and left behind a man who knows what it feels like to earn every ounce of progress.

Over Two Decades of Consistency

And I never stopped. For over two decades now, I've been consistent in training and nutrition. Day after day. Year after year. No excuses.

The truth is this: fitness isn't just about the body. It's about the mind. Research shows that when you train, you release endorphins (your brain's natural "feel-good" chemicals), lower cortisol levels (your stress hormone), and increase resilience against both physical and psychological stressors. Clinical studies have demonstrated that exercise isn't just about aesthetics; it rewires your brain, boosts mood, and sharpens focus.

That's why fitness is the healthiest outlet there is. Physical fitness and mental fitness go hand in hand. I've faced failures and struggles where I could have turned to alcohol, drugs or self pity, but instead I turned to the gym. The iron never judged me. The iron never let me down.

Discipline Separates the Great

The greatest athletes understood this. Michael Jordan said, *"I've always believed that if you put in the work, the results will come."*

Kobe Bryant lived what he called the Mamba Mentality: an obsession with discipline and relentless consistency.

They weren't casual about their craft. They were fanatics. Obsessed. Religious in their routines. That's what made them great. Discipline separated them from everyone else.

But you don't have to be Kobe or Jordan to see the truth: discipline and structure are what separate the good from the great, and the great from the greatest.

Your Body, Your Temple

Your body is your temple. Treat it like one. Be proud of it. The way you care for your body reflects who you are: disciplined, consistent, committed. Some of the most successful people I know are also the most physically fit, not by coincidence, but because **how you do one thing is how you do everything.** They're obsessive about training, diet, work, relationships, and success. That wiring makes them relentless.

Some of the best, hardest decisions of my life weren't made in a boardroom, they were made under a barbell, or in the heat of the sauna.

And if you're reading this and feel behind in life, it's not too late. You can rewire yourself. Start with your body and your mind. Then move forward.

Muscle = Longevity

Building muscle isn't just about flexing in the mirror or landing smoking hot babes. Sure, confidence comes with it, but here's the real kicker: **muscle is directly tied to longevity.**

This isn't bro-science, it's actual clinical data. Studies have consistently shown that older adults with higher levels of muscle mass live longer, healthier lives. In fact, muscle mass has been identified as a **predictor of mortality**, meaning more muscle = lower risk of dying early. Sarcopenia (age-related muscle loss) is linked with frailty, falls, fractures, disability, and premature death *(Mitchell et al., 2012; Rosenberg, 2019)*.

Think about it: when you hit your 60s, 70s, 80s, the last thing you want is to be fragile. Muscle is what keeps you mobile, independent, and resilient. It protects your bones, improves metabolic health, and even reduces the risk of chronic diseases like type 2 diabetes and heart disease *(Basaria et al., 2010)*.

So when I'm training, I'm not just stacking plates for aesthetics. I'm literally building a longer runway for my life. More muscle means more time, time to move, time to live, time to enjoy the people I love.

Muscle isn't vanity.

Muscle is medicine.

Muscle is longevity.

Movement Is a Gift

If you are reading this book and are able to move, **have gratitude.**

Movement is one of the greatest gifts we take for granted. As a hospitalist physician, I've seen too many patients who lost this gift, either through congenital conditions or sudden tragedy.

Imagine your life as a quadriplegic or paraplegic, depending on others 24/7 just to eat, bathe, or get out of bed. Suddenly, every step, every stretch, every workout feels like a blessing. They wish for the very thing so many of us take for granted.

If you can get up out of bed, if you can read these words, if you can move your body even a little, you are blessed. Movement is a gift. Don't wait until it's gone to realize that.

Movement is medicine. Movement is purpose. Movement is life.

Patient Story #1: The Stroke Survivor

One of my patients was a lifelong athlete in his 50s. A massive stroke left him unable to move the entire right side of his body. Overnight, he went from running marathons to being trapped in his own body. But he refused to quit. With relentless physical therapy, sheer willpower, and faith, he slowly regained function.

The day he stood and took his first unassisted steps, he looked at me and said:

> *"Every step I take now feels like freedom. I will never take another step for granted again."*

That line broke me. He didn't just regain his mobility; he reclaimed his life.

Patient Story #2: The Car Accident Survivor

Another patient was a young mother in her 30s who was hit by a car while biking. The accident shattered her pelvis and left her unable to walk for months. Her independence was gone. But she fought. Through surgeries, rehab, and months of pain, she rebuilt herself step by step.

The first time she walked back into my clinic unassisted, tears streaming down her face, she said:

> *"When I was lying in that hospital bed, I thought I'd never be able to tuck my kids into bed again, never be able to chase them in the park, never be able to stand on my own two feet and cook a meal for my family. But today, walking in here, I realized something: these legs aren't just mine; they're a gift. And I will use them every single day for as long as God allows."*

I cried like a child who found out Santa wasn't real.

Pay It Forward

Fitness didn't just make me better; it gave me a bigger purpose. Through my own journey, I've been able to motivate, inspire, and improve the lives of others. There's no greater reward than seeing someone live healthier, stronger, and more purposeful because of a spark you lit.

The fact that I can help people step into their best selves only deepens my love for fitness. It turns this from a personal passion into a mission. And here's the truth: if you are lucky and blessed enough to find your passion, don't keep it to yourself. Use it to help others the same way it helped you.

That's when passion stops being just a hobby and becomes something greater, a force for change, a legacy. That, my friend, is beautiful.

The Challenge

So here's my challenge to you: for the next 30 days, move your body every single day. No excuses, no half-ass attempts, no "I'll start Monday". I don't care if it's lifting, running, walking, yoga, or crawling across your living room floor, just move.

Track it. Own it. Live it.

By the end of those 30 days, you'll realize the iron doesn't just change your body; it changes your mind, your mood, your confidence, and your entire life. And if you commit to this, even when you don't feel like it, you'll have something most people never get: proof that discipline works.

Because at the end of the day, fitness isn't just about saving my life, it's about helping you save yours.

> *"Fitness didn't just build my body; it helped build my life. And if you let it, it can build yours too."*
>
> — Adam Rajoulh, MD

Chapter 5

Nutrition And Gut Health

"Let food be thy medicine and medicine be thy food."

— Hippocrates

Food as Fuel

You can have the sexiest Lamborghini in your driveway, but if you fill it with the wrong fuel, it won't run. Your body works the same way. It doesn't matter how disciplined your workouts are, how optimized your supplement stack is, or how cutting-edge your recovery devices are, if your nutrition is garbage, your performance and your health will be too.

Nutrition is the foundation. It's the most important lever we have for health, prevention, and longevity. In my medical practice, I've seen countless cases where disease could have been avoided altogether if nutrition had been prioritized. Yet as a society, we wait until disease develops, then we throw pills at it. That's not medicine, that's damage control.

Hippocrates knew 400 years before Christ what we still can't seem to figure out today: food is the foundation of health. We spend billions treating disease, but too little preventing it.

A Healthy Relationship With Food

Before anything else, your relationship with food has to be right. It should be like your relationship with your spouse, healthy, supportive, and something you actually enjoy. And just like marriage, if food keeps you miserable, bloated, and broke... you're probably in the wrong relationship.

I don't even like the word *diet*. Ever notice it has the word *die* in it?

Food isn't supposed to kill you.

It's supposed to fuel, heal, and sustain you. The word *diet* gives some people the *"ick"*, and for good reason.

Having a healthy relationship is not about **quantity**, it's about **quality**. The same principle applies to food. This is why I don't buy into obsessively counting calories. While it may help some people, it's not the whole picture.

Take this example: one apple is about the same calories as 15 Sour Patch Kids. Fifteen! But we all know those two are not created equal. One is packed with fiber, vitamins, antioxidants and water. The other is basically sugar in a Halloween costume. This is exactly what I mean when I say the *source* is everything.

Instead of chasing calorie numbers, focus on the **quality** of your food. Choose nutrient-dense options that support your body rather than inflame it. That means omega-3 rich foods, vitamin B12 sources, and proteins that are lower in hormones and antibiotics.

Think grass-fed, pasture-raised meats, organic poultry and eggs, and wild-caught fish. Balance this with plenty of colorful plant foods: fruits, vegetables, and legumes to cover your micronutrient bases and support overall health.

So, don't just count calories, make your calories *count*.

Food should be flexible, not a prison sentence. Build a relationship with it that lets you live, thrive, and still enjoy life.

Balance Over Extremes

Do you think our ancestors, out hunting with their bare hands, were eating foods with preservatives they couldn't pronounce? Of course not. If it's complicated, it probably won't work.

Every few years, a new fad diet goes viral. Keto, vegan, carnivore, paleo: each claim to be the holy grail. The truth is they all have benefits, but none are perfect. Companies and influencers overcomplicate eating because confusion sells products. It's marketing. It's pseudoscience. It's a money grab.

Dieting is simple. Even animals know how to "diet." Lions don't hire nutritionists. Birds don't measure macros. Yet humans, with all our "superfoods," detox teas, and calorie calculators, manage to make eating more confusing than astrophysics.

And please, spare me the influencers. You don't need a soccer mom on TikTok telling you to drink a gallon of apple cider vinegar or a teenager hawking the latest "detox blend" of overpriced herbs. Save your money.

And let me be clear: I'm an advocate of red meat. It's been a staple since prehistoric times. Our ancestors didn't survive on soy patties or neon colored snack cakes, they thrived on animal protein, fire, and grit.

Nutrition science keeps evolving, so follow the data, not the dogma.

Keep It Simple: Real Food Wins

If it comes in a shiny package with cartoon mascots and a chemical list that reads like a pharmacy inventory, leave it on the shelf. The middle aisles of the grocery store are a trap, sprinkles, seed oils, corn syrup, and preservatives dressed up as food.

Stick with:

- **Protein first.** Meat, eggs, fish, dairy if tolerated. Protein builds muscle, balances hormones, and keeps you full.
- **Whole plants.** Fruits and vegetables, colorful, simple, nutrient dense. And don't forget fiber. Fiber helps regulate digestion, supports gut bacteria, and keeps you satisfied longer.
- **Healthy fats.** Avocados, nuts, olive oil. Not hydrogenated industrial oils.

That's it. You don't need a PhD in nutrition to figure this out.

And if I had to pick a diet that best matches the way I eat, it would be the Mediterranean diet. I'm not totally against carbs, but I believe in prioritizing meals around protein, keeping carbs lower, and filling the rest with whole fruits, vegetables, and fiber. Simple, balanced, sustainable.

And John Cena kept it even simpler: *"If it breathes or if it's green, eat it."* That's about as close as you'll get to common-sense nutrition advice from a WWE superstar.

Protein Is King

Undisputed. King.

Protein isn't just for bodybuilders flexing in the mirror. It's the foundation of life. Nearly every major chemical reaction in your body depends on it, from building muscle to repairing tissues, from making enzymes to producing hormones and neurotransmitters.

All your meals, breakfast, lunch, dinner, even snacks, should be prioritized around protein. Current recommendations for active adults are 1.4–2.0 grams of protein per kilogram of body weight per day, far higher than the outdated minimums printed on food labels.

And no, this isn't just because I'm a "protein bro." You know the stereotype: the meathead in the gym yelling *"Protein! Protein! More protein!"* Well... guilty as charged. But here's the difference, there's real science behind it. Protein boosts metabolism, improves insulin sensitivity (stabilizes blood sugar), reduces hunger, preserves muscle, and extends longevity.

Skip protein, and you'll feel it everywhere, in the gym, at work, even in your mood.

Protein isn't optional. Protein is king.

Portion Control and Timing

- **Calories are king.** Weight loss = deficit. Weight gain = surplus. Period. It's physics, not voodoo.
- **Front-load your meals.** Larger portions earlier in the day, when metabolism is higher, beat heavy meals at night. Eating a giant dinner right before bed is like filling your gas tank before parking for the night, pointless.

- **Smaller, frequent meals.** Spread throughout the day, they stabilize energy, help regulate appetite, and prevent the late night binge.
- **Cut the junk.** Processed foods, seed oils, and sugary drinks don't belong on the menu if performance and longevity are your goals.

Intermittent Fasting

Intermittent fasting isn't a fad, it's one of the oldest health practices in human history, with modern science finally catching up. I practice intermittent fasting once or twice a week. You don't need to do it daily, but the benefits are real:

- Improves **insulin sensitivity** and metabolic health
- Supports **cognition and focus**
- Boosts **immunity**
- Promotes **longevity** through cellular cleanup processes like autophagy.

And unlike extreme cleanses or 72-hour starvation stunts, intermittent fasting is sustainable and well-researched.

Do you need to starve yourself for a week, let your body wither, and call it "health"? No. That's insanity. Yet there are people online telling you to do exactly that. If you want medical advice from a guy named Stan playing Fortnite on YouTube, be my guest. But as a physician, I don't recommend it.

Hydration: More Than Water

"Drink more water" is good advice, but incomplete. Hydration is about balance. Electrolytes, sodium, potassium, magnesium, keep your nerves firing and muscles contracting. That's why athletes, soldiers, and high performers supplement electrolytes: hydration is performance. Before you go to war, in the gym, at work, or in life, you fuel your body with the right hydration.

This is why I start my mornings with cold water mixed with full spectrum electrolytes.

Superfoods That Actually Work

Forget the marketing hype. A handful of foods actually pull their weight:

- **Steak:** arguably the most nutrient-dense food on the planet, providing protein, iron, zinc, selenium, phosphorus, magnesium, potassium, chromium, copper, B vitamins, vitamin A, D, and K2, creatine, carnosine, taurine, CoQ10, CLA and more. It's a prehistoric superfood, and it still fuels peak performance today.
- **Turmeric:** Natural anti-inflammatory that supports brain and joint health.
- **Pineapple:** Contains bromelain, an enzyme that aids digestion and reduces inflammation.
- **Beets:** Rich in betaine and nitrates, improving blood flow and athletic performance.
- **Avocados & nuts:** Packed with monounsaturated fats for brain and heart health.

- **Fermented foods:** Yogurt, sauerkraut, kefir, kimchi, support gut microbiota, which in turn boost immunity and mood.
- **Apple cider vinegar:** Can modestly improve blood sugar, but it's not going to give you six-pack abs.

The Brain–Gut Axis

Up to 90–95% of serotonin, your "happy hormone", is produced in the gut, not the brain. That means mood, clarity, and resilience all hinge on your microbiome.

When your gut is trashed by preservatives, fried foods, and seed oils, serotonin production plummets. Dysbiosis sets in, leaving you foggy, depressed, and drained. But when you fuel your microbiome with whole foods and fermented foods, your brain lights up. Focus sharpens. Mood stabilizes. Stress becomes easier to carry.

And let's be real: you don't even need a scientific paper to tell you this. Have you ever noticed when you eat like crap, you feel like crap? That's your brain–gut axis doing its thing. Cheat meals are fine, everyone has them, but there's a reason I feel like garbage every time I order a mountain of hot wings, crush a greasy pizza, or dive into a tub of neon colored ice cream. Your gut doesn't lie. When you feed it junk, it sends the bill straight to your brain in the form of fatigue, brain fog, and regret.

Your body is smarter than you think. It's constantly giving you feedback. Pay attention.

Avoid the Poison

If there's one universal rule of nutrition, it's this: avoid toxins disguised as food.

- **Nicotine:** Addictive, damages cardiovascular health, carcinogenic, wrecks performance.
- **Alcohol:** Destroys sleep, hormones, and recovery. It literally blunts muscle protein synthesis, translation: it kills your gym gains.
- **Seed oils (soybean, corn, canola, sunflower):** Highly processed, pro-inflammatory, linked to metabolic dysfunction.
- **Ultra-processed vegan foods:** If you're vegan for personal reasons, fine, but don't assume "vegan" means healthy. Many are packed with preservatives and lab chemicals, some that I can't even pronounce.

A Note on Caffeine & Sugar

Not all "villains" are created equal. Caffeine and sugar aren't evil, in fact, both can serve a purpose in the right dose. Caffeine, in moderation, improves alertness, focus, and even exercise performance. But slam down energy drinks like they're water, and you'll wreck your sleep, jack up your cortisol, and tank recovery.

Sugar? Same deal. Your body actually needs glucose for energy, especially in high-intensity training. But the problem isn't sugar itself, it's the chronic, excessive intake from sodas, candy, processed snacks, and hidden syrups in everything. Small amounts in whole foods like fruit are fine. The issue is mainlining sugar like it's fuel for a NASCAR pit stop.

The Truth About Testosterone

To juice or not to juice?

I'm an 80's baby so I grew up on Stallone and Schwarzenegger movies. They had action figure physiques. They were monsters. I'm sure I'm not the only male who was tempted to dabble with anabolic steroids after watching their movies. Thankfully, I never did it.

Testosterone is the primary male hormone, essential for muscle mass, bone strength, energy, and libido. It's normal for levels to decline gradually after age 30, usually a few percent each year. That's not a disease, it's biology. For men with hypogonadism or medically low testosterone, **testosterone replacement therapy (TRT)** may be indicated.

Here's the catch: in otherwise healthy men with normal levels, abusing testosterone or anabolic steroids isn't just unnecessary, it's dangerous. Studies show that misuse increases risk of liver failure, hypertension, heart failure and even strokes (Basaria et al., 2010). I've seen these effects myself in my clinical practice.

Yet many chase testosterone like a shortcut to energy, size, or sexual vitality. The truth? It's just not worth it. Remember, the most important aspect for improving your health or body composition comes down to two elements: your *diet and movement.* Nobody can argue this. Period. It's all about long term results. Again, unless you are truly deficient, hormones are just not worth it. Sustainable health is built on long term habits, not quick fixes.

Preventative Medicine

Here's the brutal truth: most of what I see in hospitals is preventable. Diabetes, hypertension, strokes, heart disease, all accelerated or caused outright by poor nutrition. Yet instead of prevention, we manage decline.

And if you want proof of how broken the system is, just look at the food served in our institutions:

- Schools: processed, sugary junk that sets kids up for obesity.
- Prisons: cheap, inflammatory, nutrient-poor food.
- Hospitals: yes, even in cardiac units, patients recovering from heart surgery are served fried food and corn syrup.

This isn't an accident. It's corporate control.

Big Food and Big Pharma

Big Food and Big Pharma combined represent a market worth **over $10 trillion a year**, two of the most powerful industries shaping global health. And here's the uncomfortable truth: Big Food and Big Pharma thrive on the same business model.

Both systems don't profit by solving and treating the root of disease. Big Food sells products that make us sick. Big Pharma sells products that manage that sickness. It's good business. *A patient cured is a customer lost.* That's why ingredients banned in Europe are still in American food, not because they're safe, but because they're profitable. Good ol' corporate America.

Medicine is science. Medicine is art. Medicine is a privilege. Medicine should NEVER be a business.

The system isn't designed to keep you healthy. It's designed to keep you alive just long enough to keep paying. That's not medicine. That's business.

"Big Food does not care about American people."

— Adam Rajoulh, MD

Chapter 6

Kill Stress Before It Kills You

"It's not the weight of the load that breaks you down, it's the way you carry it."

— Lou Holtz

Stress: The Silent Killer

Stress isn't just annoying, it's deadly. Chronic stress has become a full-blown public health crisis. More than half of Americans live under persistent stress (American Psychological Association, 2022). The American Medical Association estimates that stress is a primary factor in more than 60 percent of all illness and disease.

Stress causes inflammation. Inflammation is the root of all disease. Heart disease, depression, diabetes, autoimmune conditions, stress doesn't discriminate. It seeps into every system of the body and quietly accelerates decline.

Why so destructive? Because stress hijacks your physiology. When you're under pressure, the sympathetic nervous system slams the panic button, fight-or-flight. Adrenaline surges. Cortisol rises. Blood pressure spikes. Blood sugar floods your bloodstream. Short term, this reaction can save your life. Long term, it erodes your health, your relationships, and your sanity.

The Hidden Costs of Stress

- **Hormonal chaos:** Chronic cortisol wrecks sleep, metabolism, and immune defense (NIH, 2021).
- **Cardiac risk:** Stress doubles your chance of heart attack or stroke (CDC, 2020).
- **Mental fallout:** Anxiety, depression, and burnout thrive in chronic stress.
- **Inflammation driver:** Stress fuels systemic inflammation, the root of cancer, autoimmune disease, and accelerated aging.

Stress is often called the "#1 proxy killer" because it doesn't just ruin health on its own, it fuels almost every other condition we fear.

You Are in Control

Here's the good news: you can't always control the storm, but you can control the sails. Stress isn't defined by what happens to you. It's defined by how you respond.

The most important thing to remember about stress is YOU are in control of how you respond to stress!

You don't need a guru or a Himalayan retreat to beat stress. Below are some science-backed, field-tested tactics that actually work.

Breathwork and the Power of Oxygen

Oxygen is life. Every cell in your body depends on it to generate energy through ATP, and without it, survival is measured in minutes. The more efficiently you deliver and use oxygen, the sharper your mind, the stronger your performance, and the calmer your stress response.

Breathwork trains this system, improving lung efficiency, circulation, and mental clarity.

Even elite athletes go to extreme lengths to boost oxygen delivery, some have even risked careers with blood doping to increase red blood cell count. Why? Because more oxygen equals more performance. That same principle applies to breathwork: it naturally enhances your VO_2max, one of the strongest predictors of endurance and resilience. The difference? Breathwork is safe, legal, and you won't have to explain to grandma why you got banned from the Olympics.

Breath Work Expansion

Breath work isn't black magic. It's physiology. Slow, controlled breathing activates the parasympathetic nervous system, lowering heart rate, cortisol (stress hormone) and blood pressure.

A study in *Frontiers in Human Neuroscience* (Zaccaro et al., 2018) found that deep diaphragmatic breathing improves emotional regulation and reduces anxiety by increasing vagal tone (your body's "calm switch").

Try This (Box Breathing):
1. Inhale for 4 seconds.
2. Hold for 4 seconds.
3. Exhale for 4 seconds.
4. Hold for 4 seconds.

(Repeat for 3–5 minutes.)

Navy SEALs use this before combat. If it can calm a soldier in a firefight, it can calm you before your Zoom meeting or spending the day with your in-laws.

Grounding: Nature's Reset Button

Grounding, or "earthing," is the practice of making direct skin contact with the Earth, like walking barefoot on grass, sand, or soil. Early studies suggest this connection may help reduce stress and inflammation by allowing the body to absorb electrons that neutralize free radicals (Chevalier et al., 2015). In one trial, people who slept on grounded mats showed healthier cortisol rhythms, better sleep, and less pain (Ghaly & Teplitz, 2004).

While more research is needed, the message is clear: spending time connected to the Earth calms both body and mind. Grounding is free, accessible, and reminds us that mental fitness doesn't always come from high-tech fixes, sometimes it's as simple as taking your shoes off and letting nature do the work it's been doing for humans for millennia.

Rewire Your Mindset

Your first step to deal with stress is to train your brain to scan for blessings, not just problems. *Gratitude* rewires neural pathways and boosts dopamine and serotonin. Translation: less whining, more winning.

Cut Out Toxic People

Energy vampires exist, and they're draining you. Replace the constant drama with people who actually bring momentum and positivity.

Remember, your network is your net worth.

Eat Smart

Prioritize protein, stick to whole foods and avoid processed foods. Cut down caffeine and sugar. Sugar gives a short term high, then slams you into inflammation, mood crashes, and insulin spikes. Stress eating Oreos feels great… until your jeans and blood pressure disagree.

Step Into the Sun

Sunlight boosts vitamin D, aligns your circadian rhythm, and improves mood. Seasonal affective disorder isn't "fake sadness." It's your biology begging for sunlight.

Volunteer and Serve

Serving others resets perspective. Stress shrinks when you realize your problems aren't the only ones in the world and that many people have bigger problems.

Prioritize Sleep

Seven to eight hours isn't luxury, it's survival. Without sleep, cortisol skyrockets, your mood tanks, and your brain operates like a drunk college kid.

Practice Mindfulness

Meditation, prayer, or even music lowers cortisol and improves emotional resilience. Think of it as antivirus software for your brain.

Exercise Like Your Life Depends On It

Because it does. Exercise reduces anxiety, strengthens your heart, and floods your brain with endorphins. It's the closest thing to legal drugs, and the side effect is abs and confidence.

Seek Professional Help

If stress is overwhelming or if there is a family history of mental illness, see a physician. Strength isn't pretending you're fine, it's knowing when to get help.

Final Thoughts on Stress

Stress isn't going anywhere. Inflation, relationships, careers, health, life will always apply pressure. But whether stress breaks you or builds you depends entirely on your response.

It's not about eliminating stress. It's about mastering it.

> "The most important thing to remember about stress is that YOU are in control of your stress."
>
> — Adam Rajoulh, MD

Chapter 7

Don't Sleep On Sleep

"Sleep is the golden chain that ties health and our bodies together."

— Thomas Dekker

Sleep: The Most Underrated Power Tool

Diet and exercise are both emphasized as the holy grail of health. But here's the uncomfortable truth: you can train like an Olympian and eat like a monk, yet if your sleep is trash, you're fighting uphill with no gas in the tank.

The CDC estimates that 1 in 3 Americans don't get adequate sleep. That's nearly 100 million people walking around sleep-deprived, essentially a nation of zombies. And no, chugging iced lattes at 4 PM doesn't make up for it.

Sleep isn't wasted time. It's the ultimate performance enhancer: resetting hormones, restoring energy, and repairing tissue every night. It's the cheapest, most underrated power tool we've got.

The Forgotten Pillar of Health

As a physician, I tell patients constantly: you can eat perfectly and train like a beast, but if you're not sleeping properly, you're sabotaging your recovery, your growth, and your longevity. Sleep is when your body hits reset, repairing cells, consolidating memory, balancing hormones, and recharging your immune system.

Neglect it, and you're basically trying to run a supercar on sugar water.

Quality Over Quantity

I've had patients tell me: "Doc, I sleep 9 or 10 hours a night, but I still wake up exhausted." Why? Because hours in bed ≠ quality sleep. Deep, restorative sleep is where the magic happens, hormones balance, the brain files away memories, and the immune system recharges. Without enough deep and REM sleep, you wake up foggy, irritable, and ready to snap at whoever cuts you off in traffic.

The Myth of Sleep Debt

I hear people tell me they'll "catch up on sleep over the weekend" like it's a game of Mario Kart. The problem is, your brain doesn't work like a bank account. You can't withdraw six hours every night, then dump in twelve on Saturday and expect to be even. Research shows that while some alertness and mood can recover with extra sleep, the deep REM stages that repair memory, learning, and emotional balance are permanently lost once missed (Van Dongen et al., *Sleep*, 2003).

Chronic partial sleep deprivation accumulates like compound interest, only in the wrong direction. After just one week of sleeping six hours per night, people perform as poorly on cognitive tests as if they'd been awake for 48 hours straight. The kicker? Most participants in those studies swore they were doing "fine," proving that sleep deprivation impairs not only performance but self- awareness of that performance (Belenky et al., *Sleep*, 2003).

Bottom line: you can't out-hustle biology. Consistency is the cure. Treat bedtime like a non-negotiable meeting with your future self. Protect it the way you'd protect your paycheck, because once lost, deep sleep is one investment you can never fully recover.

Sleep, Mood and Immunity

Sleep isn't just recovery, it's one of the most powerful medicines you'll ever take. During deep sleep, your immune system goes to work, releasing cytokines that fight infection and repair tissue. Studies show that a single night of restricted sleep can reduce natural killer (NK) cell activity by up to 70%, leaving you more vulnerable to illness (Irwin et al., *Psychosom Med*, 1994). Chronic sleep deprivation doesn't just increase your chance of catching a cold, it raises your long-term risk of heart disease, diabetes, and even shortened lifespan.

Sleep also regulates mood by balancing neurotransmitters like serotonin and dopamine. That's why even one rough night can make you more irritable, anxious, or prone to stress. Over time, poor sleep is strongly linked to depression and anxiety disorders (Walker, *Why We Sleep*, 2017).

The Ripple Effect of Poor Sleep

Here's what happens when sleep tanks:

- Hormones go haywire (leptin and ghrelin = more cravings, more fat).
- Immune defenses weaken (hello, every seasonal cold).
- Mental health suffers (higher depression, anxiety, irritability).
- Reaction times slow (car accidents skyrocket).
- Memory and focus nosedive.
- Testosterone crashes. Libido follows.

Poor sleep isn't just "feeling groggy." It's like trying to rebuild a house with no blueprint and no workers. Eventually, everything falls apart.

Sleep and Longevity

Sleep isn't just about how sharp you feel tomorrow, it's an insurance policy for your long term health. Chronic poor sleep is linked to:

- Heart disease (AHA, 2020)
- Obesity and diabetes (NIH, 2019)
- Alzheimer's disease (NIA, 2020)
- Shortened lifespan

From a resilience perspective, sleep is non-negotiable. Without it, your physical defenses weaken, your emotional stability crumbles, and your ability to handle stress vanishes. With it, you don't just recover, you build armor. Sleep protects your immune system, sharpens your mind, and extends your health span, giving you more years of quality life.

Flip it around, and prioritizing sleep becomes one of the most powerful anti-aging "drugs" on the planet, and it's free.

Sleep Apnea: The Silent Killer

Here's a condition I've seen ruin lives more than people realize: obstructive sleep apnea (OSA). Obesity is the number one risk factor. In the United States, 42 percent of adults are obese, which translates to roughly 110 to 115 million people. An estimated 30 million American adults have obstructive sleep apnea, but most don't even know it. Only about 6 million are actually diagnosed.

What it does is brutal, your airway collapses during sleep, your oxygen plummets, and your body jolts awake dozens of times an hour since your body is in fight or flight mode instead of rest mode. Translation: you never get true deep sleep.

Think about that, your brain and body are basically suffocating in slow motion while you "sleep." No wonder it's linked to heart attacks, strokes, arrhythmias, diabetes, and cognitive decline.

Red flags:
- Loud snoring
- Pauses in breathing or gasping for air
- Waking up exhausted despite "enough" hours in bed
- Daytime fatigue, brain fog, or nodding off at stoplights

Here's a personal story. At a buddy's bachelor party, I was rooming with one of my childhood friends. First night, the guy starts snoring so loud it could've been heard in Afghanistan. Then I notice he's gasping like a fish out of water. I told him point-blank: "Bro, you've got sleep apnea. Get tested."

Sure enough, he was diagnosed with **severe** sleep apnea. He got fitted with a CPAP, and overnight his energy improved, his libido came back, and his mood got better (well… he went from *unpleasant* to *barely bearable*, progress is progress). Sleep didn't just save his nights; it saved his life.

Take-home: if you snore, gasp, or wake up tired no matter how long you're in bed, stop ignoring it. Get tested. If you don't have any of these symptoms but are obese or overweight, STILL get tested. A sleep test is noninvasive and painless. A CPAP might not look sexy but neither does a stroke.

Healthy Sleep Hygiene

Here's the good news: you don't need fancy supplements or biohacks to improve your sleep. What you need is structure, habits that sync your body's natural circadian rhythm.

Sleep Hygiene Blueprint (Doctor's Orders)

- **Consistency is King**, same bedtime, same wake-up.
- **Dark**, blackout curtains, eye masks, or dim lights.
- **Cool it Down**, 65–68°F (18–20°C) = prime sleep zone.
- **Ca eine Cuto** , no caffeine after 2 PM (or at least 6-8 hours before bedtime)
- **Screen Detox**, no blue light/screens 1–2 hrs before bed.
- **Wind-Down Ritual**, stretching, journaling, prayer, or reading.
- **Workout Smart**, finish training at least 2 hrs before bed.
- **Skip the Nightcap**, alcohol knocks you out but wrecks REM.

- **Natural Support (optional)**, magnesium glycinate, chamomile, L-theanine, valerian root, 5-HTP, Vitamin B6. Safer than prescription sleep meds for most people.

Why Sleep Comes First

Athletes, soldiers, and executives rely on strict sleep hygiene since performance collapses without them. Reaction time, focus, and emotional stability all tank when sleep is cut short. In fact, some military research shows that a single all-nighter can impair cognitive function as much as a 0.1% blood alcohol level, legally drunk.

Here's the truth bomb I tell patients: **fix sleep before you fix anything else.**

Bottom line: sleep is the cheapest performance enhancing drug you'll ever take. Respect it, protect it, and it will repay you with energy, clarity, and resilience.

You can't out train bad sleep. You can't out diet chronic sleep deprivation. If you want muscle, fat loss, focus, or better health and mood, the foundation is sleep. Without it, everything else crumbles.

> "Sleep isn't weakness, it's the weapon that reloads your body and mind for war."
>
> — Adam Rajoulh, MD

Chapter 8

The Power Protocol

"The measure of a man is what he does with power."

— Plato

What Is Power?

Power is the ability to influence your environment, outcomes, or other people. Power isn't just politics, money, or control over others. Power is the ability to act. It's not just about dominance, it's about capacity. The capacity to shape your own life, to withstand resistance, and to influence outcomes.

Psychologists define power as the capacity to shape behavior, your own and others'. In physiology, power is force multiplied by velocity: not just strength, but strength applied fast. And in life, power is discipline in action, doing what you said you'd do, even when you don't feel like it.

But here's the truth: real power isn't about controlling other people. It's about controlling yourself. **Discipline and self-mastery are the highest forms of power.** If you can master your mind, your body, your habits, and your daily choices, you become unstoppable.

That's why the *Power Protocol* matters. It's not a gimmick, not a "hack," not another guru checklist. It's the blueprint for mastering yourself, one pillar at a time.

The Power Protocol, Five Pillars

Systems beat goals. Goals are about results, but systems are about the processes that lead to results. Systems of daily practice are what lead to desired outcomes.

<u>The Power Protocol is your blueprint for health, power and purpose.</u>

This protocol isn't complicated. It doesn't need to be. It's five simple pillars that you can actually implement. The bottom line, do everything with **PURPOSE.**

When you wake up, eat, work, and train, do it all with purpose.

1. **Morning Mindset Protocol**

    Gratitude, push-ups, breath work, sunlight, grounding, cold showers

    (See Chapter 3)

2. **Nutrition Protocol**

    Hydration, electrolytes, whole foods, protein first, intermittent fasting, fuel over comfort

    (See Chapter 5)

3. **Training Protocol**

    Consistency, Heavy resistance compound lifts (squats, deadlifts, presses) with varied movements, heat/cold therapy, no skipped leg days

    (See Chapter 4)

4. **Sleep Protocol**

    Rest as a weapon

    (See Chapter 7)

5. **Stress Protocol**

    Managing pressure before it destroys you.

    (See Chapter 6)

These aren't hacks. They're habits.

Discipline is a lifestyle, not a vibe or a mood.

Pillar #1, Morning Mindset Protocol

Most people wake up stressed, immediately reaching for their phone and diving into the chaos. Bills, work, relationships, stressors, it all hits before your day even starts. Congrats, you have already lost.

The state above is a **low vibration**, and when you begin the day with low vibrational energy, you carry it forward. This isn't just an idea; it's physics. Research from the HeartMath Institute and others shows that emotions carry measurable frequencies, and gratitude, love, and joy produce coherence in the heart and brain. This coherence improves focus, resilience, and even positively influences those around you.

Start strong. Start your day with a high vibration. The easiest and quickest way to do this is through *gratitude*.

Gratitude rewires your brain. Studies in neuroplasticity show that gratitude practices increase activity in regions tied to resilience and emotion regulation. It literally builds mental armor.

Every morning, I thank God for my life, my health, my daughter, my family, and my purpose. Starting my day with gratitude sets the pace for the rest of the day.

Then I put my body in motion: 100 push-ups right after my feet touch the floor. This is followed by breath work (box breathing 4-4- 4-4) outside in the sun. Grounding is optional but an added bonus which I try to do at least a few times a week. Some mornings, I'll take a cold shower to keep me alert.

It's not about perfection; it's about ritual. Ritual that forces presence, gratitude, and discipline before the world demands anything.

Morning Rituals That Prime the Day

- **Gratitude & Reflection**: Naming blessings first thing rewires your default state toward optimism and high vibrational energy.
- **Sunlight Exposure**: Getting outside for natural light within 30 minutes of waking resets circadian rhythm, improves energy, and sets you up for deeper sleep later. Grounding is an added weapon. Mother Nature is healing.
- **Breath Work**: Improves emotional regulation and reduces anxiety by increasing vagal tone (your body's "calm switch")
- **Movement**: A quick set of pushups and walking outside shifts physiology from stagnation to activation.
- **Cold Showers/Sauna**: forces adaptation, boosts norepinephrine, sharpens alertness, and conditions you to embrace discomfort.

(See Chapter 3 for more on gratitude and mindset)

Pillar #2, Nutrition Protocol

Start your day with 8–16 oz cold water + full spectrum electrolytes (Celtic sea salt, magnesium glycinate, potassium)

Your brain runs on minerals as much as it runs on calories.

Nutrition is fuel, not comfort. Focus on nutrient-dense meals over mindless snacking and junk food. Quality over quantity.

Research shows interment fasting supports cognition, immunity, metabolism, and even longevity.

Fuel the machine. Don't feed the craving.

The Two Essentials:

1. Stick to whole foods.

   Avoid preserved and processed foods at all costs.

2. Prioritize protein at every meal (1.4–2.0 g/kg/day)

These are the only rules I consider **absolutes**. Everything else is flexible.

(See Chapter 5 for more on nutrition and gut health)

Pillar #3, Training Protocol

Discipline over motivation. Training isn't about chasing feelings, it's about keeping promises.

My philosophy: confuse the body, avoid plateaus, and hit failure. Heavy compound movements first (squats, deadlifts, presses) followed by varied lighter accessory work after, upper/lower split daily, variation monthly. No skipped leg days. Ever.

The truth is there's no perfect workout, just like there's no perfect diet. Everybody wants the new hack, the secret exercise, the magic solution, the new Ozempic. There isn't one. Progress comes down to consistency, intensity, and adaptation over time.

Training smart means respecting recovery, shocking the body with variation, and never just going through the motions. Fast-twitch fibers are the key. Sports science shows that explosive, high-intensity work activates these fibers, which drive adaptation, growth, and athletic power.

No matter what your routine looks like, the principle is simple:

when you train, train with *purpose*.

Heat as a Weapon

Sauna therapy is one of the simplest but most underrated recovery tools. Heat exposure triggers heat shock proteins, repairing cells and boosting resilience. A 20-year Finnish study found sauna users cut their risk of cardiac mortality by up to 52%.

I use the sauna almost daily after training. Not just for the science, but because it resets me. It's where I can pray and clear my head. Stress melts. Clarity returns.

The principle is simple: use heat (or cold) as a tool to adapt and come back stronger.

(See Chapter 4 for more on training)

Pillar #4, Sleep Protocol

Sleep isn't weakness. **It's the ultimate performance enhancer.**

You cannot out train a poor sleep schedule.

Sleep regulates hormones, repairs tissue, consolidates memory, and restores willpower. Studies show people sleeping less than 6 hours a night face higher risks of obesity, depression, and cardiovascular disease.

My rules are simple:
- Cool, dark, quiet room.
- Consistent bedtime
- No caffeine after 2-3 PM
- No screens in bed.

Rest is a weapon. Grind without recovery is just slow self-destruction.

(See Chapter 7 for more on sleep)

Pillar #5, Stress Protocol

Stress is inevitable. Mismanaged stress is deadly. Chronic stress rewires the brain, shrinks memory centers, and accelerates aging.

That's why I treat stress management as a daily practice. Breath work, sunlight, sauna, training, family time, all of these pull me out of fight-or-flight mode. Stress won't disappear, but you can own it before it owns you.

The most important truth about stress is this: YOU control it. It's never the setback itself that defines your outcome, it's your response.

Own your stress before it owns you. (See Chapter 6 for more on stress)

Biohacking for Longevity

"Biohacking" has become one of those Silicon Valley buzzwords that gets slapped on everything, from blue-light glasses to $30 mushroom coffee. At this point, the word is so overused it's like calling scrolling TikTok at 3 a.m. a productivity hack. The truth? Real biohacking isn't about gadgets, it's about evidence-based practices that actually improve your body and brain.

Forget the $10,000 cryo-chambers or influencer gadgets. The real biohacks are simple, science backed, and available to everyone. Biohacking isn't about turning yourself into Iron Man; it's about using proven strategies to push back aging, boost energy, and build resilience.

Intermittent fasting is one of the strongest levers. Restricting your eating window improves insulin sensitivity, lowers inflammation, and even triggers autophagy, your body's cellular "clean-up crew" that clears out damaged cells (Patterson & Sears, 2017).

Heat and cold therapy work too. Studies from Finland show that people who use sauna several times per week cut their risk of sudden cardiac death by nearly 40% (Laukkanen et al., 2015). On the flip side, cold exposure, even a daily cold shower, spikes norepinephrine, lowers inflammation, and conditions your body to handle stress.

High-intensity interval training (HIIT) is another cheat code. By pushing your body hard in short bursts, you increase mitochondrial density, the tiny power plants in your cells that keep you young.

Sleep is still perhaps the most underrated biohack. Short changing it accelerates aging and shrinks telomeres, the protective caps on your DNA (Epel et al., 2004).

Supplementation can also help but as the name implies, it is "supplemental." It doesn't replace food/nutrition

- Creatine monohydrate helps improve brain and muscle performance.
- Beta Alanine helps with endurance.
- Omega-3 fatty acids support cardiovascular and cognitive health.
- Vitamin D3/K2 supports cardiovascular, bone and immune health.
- Adaptogens, lion's mane, saffron and others help with mood and memory.
- Green tea extract (EGCG), cayenne pepper and protein (yes protein) help support fat loss.
- Collagen helps with skin and joint health.
- Lutein and niacinamide helps support skin health and photoprotection.
- Magnesium glycinate, chamomile, L-theanine, valerian root, 5-HTP help with sleep.

The list goes on...

None of the above, however, will outweigh your ***food and movement***

Primal hacks: grounding, nature exposure, and breathwork are free and should not be ignored. Walking barefoot on grass or practicing slow diaphragmatic breathing lowers cortisol and restores balance to your nervous system (Chevalier et al., 2015).

Forest bathing in Japan has been shown to drop blood pressure and stress hormones.

Positive thinking and gratitude is also key. A strong mind is the ultimate biohack. Research shows optimism lowers stress, improves cardiovascular health, and even extends lifespan. You can pop all the pills you want, but if your mindset is toxic, your body pays the price. *Mental fitness* is the foundation on which every other biohack rests.

Bottom line: Biohacking isn't about being flashy; it's about stacking small, proven wins, physical *and* mental, that keep your body younger, your mind sharper, and your resilience higher for decades to come.

Mind–Body Unity

You can have a strong body but a weak mind, or a strong mind but a weak body. Either way, you lose. Evolution demands both.

The *Power Protocol* isn't about hacks. It's about wholeness. It's about building a mind that doesn't crack under pressure and a body that doesn't break under stress.

That's true *power*.

> "Real power is self-mastery. Once you own yourself, the rest falls into place."
>
> — Adam Rajoulh, MD

Chapter 9

Failure And Resilience

"Stay Hard."

— David Goggins

Failure Is Inevitable

Failure is an absolute truth for everyone, the same way death is. There isn't a single human walking this planet who hasn't fallen flat on their face, some literally, some figuratively. The only people who claim they've never failed are liars... or they've never tried anything harder than tying their shoes.

When you face a setback, you really only have three options:

1. Do something constructive.
2. Do something destructive.
3. Do absolutely nothing.

Number three feels safe, but let's call it what it is, destruction in disguise. Doing nothing just means staying stuck while the rest of the world keeps moving forward.

Spoiler alert: the universe doesn't hand out participation trophies.

So, in reality, there's only one option: respond constructively. Failing is inevitable. Evolving from it is a choice. The former makes you human.

The latter makes you unstoppable.

Resilience: The Forgotten Muscle

Everyone wants six-pack abs, money in the bank, and a highlight reel life. But when life punches you in the face, and it will, it's not your abs, your paycheck, or your follower count that saves you. It's resilience.

As a physician, I've seen this firsthand. Patients who kept landing back in the hospital weren't always the sickest. They were the ones with the victim mentality. It was always someone else's fault, their genetics, their doctor, their bad luck. They stayed stuck.

The ones who took ownership? They made progress. They understood the truth: it's not the problem that defines your life. It's how you react to it.

Research even shows this isn't just philosophy, resilience predicts better recovery from trauma and stress-related disorders (Bonanno, 2004). It's a muscle. And like any muscle, it only grows under stress and resistance.

Programming Resilience

Resilience is more than just grit; it's mastering the dialogue between your conscious and subconscious mind. Every thought plants a seed, and life's conditions grow from those seeds. Negative or scattered thinking weakens you, while focused, harmonious thoughts build strength and direction.

The subconscious never argues, it simply acts on the ideas it's given. When you visualize, concentrate, and reaffirm purpose into your consciousness, you're programming yourself to rise after any setbacks.

Once resilience is programmed, failure loses its sting. A setback doesn't even feel like failure anymore, it's simply an event. Failure no longer breaks you. It does not define you. It doesn't even phase you. Instead, it becomes second nature to shrug off defeat and move forward, as if saying, *"Oh, hi failure we meet again? Welcome back."*

True resilience means hardship no longer defines you, it refines you.

Fear as Fuel

Fear of failure is a crippling disease that will absolutely prevent you from achieving your full potential and best version of yourself. Instead of fearing failure, welcome it with open arms and squeeze the life out of your failure to remind it that it will NOT control you and your destiny.

Fear doesn't disappear just because you get stronger, in fact, every new level of growth brings a new level of fear. Susan Jeffers, in *Feel the Fear and*

Do It Anyway, explains that courage isn't the absence of fear but the decision to act despite it. At the root of most fear is a single thought: *"I can't handle it."* The truth? You can. When you take risks, lean into discomfort, and choose action over avoidance, you don't just survive, you thrive.

Fear shrinks every time you push forward, and confidence grows in its place. As Rocky told Adonis Creed while walking him down to the ring during his championship fight: *"I'd always feel nervous at times like this but it's going to give you energy. That's normal."*

Mike Tyson quoted "Fear is the greatest obstacle to learning, but fear is your best friend. Fear will keep you alive." He often spoke about how he embraced fear before fights, not as weakness, but as energy that sharpened his instincts and performance.

The mantra is simple: *I can handle it.* When that becomes your default response, fear doesn't break you, it fuels you.

Action Step: Identify one fear you've been avoiding, a conversation, a decision, or a risk. Take one concrete step toward confronting it this week.

Courage and Resilience

Courage is not the absence of fear; it is acting despite it. Rosa Parks showed quiet yet world-shaking courage when she refused to give up her seat on a Montgomery bus in 1955. Her single act of defiance ignited a movement that reshaped history. Courage doesn't always roar on a battlefield, sometimes it whispers "no" in the face of injustice.

Resilience is the ability to get back up when life knocks you down. Nelson Mandela endured 27 years in prison, yet walked out not bitter but stronger, ready to lead a divided nation. Resilience isn't about never falling; it's about refusing to stay down.

My Own Battles

I don't preach resilience from a podium, I preach it from the trenches.

I've been physically beaten. Threatened. Broke. Canceled. Divorced. Fired. Arrested. Defamed. I've lost family. I've lost friends. I've lost myself.

I know I'll go through more hardships. That's life. But here's the secret: once you prime your body and your mind for hardship, those blows stop breaking you. They forge you.

Pain isn't something to run from. Pain is the entry fee for greatness. Every hardship I've endured has carved me into a sharper weapon, a tougher man, a stronger father, and a more grounded leader.

Thank you God for my failures. Thank you for the pain.

Thank you for making me stronger.

The World Owes You Nothing

Let's kill this delusion once and for all: *the world owes you nothing.*

Not a paycheck. Not a healthy body. Not a relationship. Not even fairness.

We live in an era of entitlement where people think they're owed comfort just for existing. That's bullshit. Nobody is coming to save you. Nobody's handing out resilience for free. You build it. You earn it through repetition, failure, and showing up on the days you don't feel like it.

Mental fitness is turning failure into fuel, not into a full stop.

Consistency Beats Talent

You can have more raw talent than anyone in the room, but without consistency, you'll lose. You can have all the motivation in the world, but without discipline, you'll crash.

You see this in fighters all the time. Muhammad Ali didn't just talk, he trained like a madman, running miles in heavy boots, sparring until exhaustion, and drilling fundamentals until they were instinct. His greatness wasn't just talent, it was consistency weaponized.

Bodybuilding taught me this. I never competed, never did it for money. But it saved my life. I was bullied as a kid for being small. Lifting weights gave me strength, confidence, and structure. Every rep in the gym translated into resilience outside the gym. That carried me through medical school, fatherhood, and life itself.

And the science agrees: consistency in training and daily habits is more predictive of long term success than raw talent alone (Duckworth et al., 2007).

Consistency isn't sexy. It's not instant. But it stays undefeated.

Victimhood vs. Ownership

We live in a society that glorifies finger pointing. Assuming personal responsibility nowadays is more rare than an honest politician. It's always someone else's fault. But here's the truth: no one is coming to save you.

Feeling sorry for oneself and living in the past has never helped anyone. It's destructive, not constructive. It's a distraction, not a solution.

Yes, trauma is real. Yes, betrayal hurts. Yes, life can be unfair. But your outcome is still your responsibility. Not your parents. Not your boss. Not your partner. You.

Ownership is power. Victimhood is poison.

Patient Story, Sickness to Spartan Races

I once treated a young man with diabetic keto acidosis in his late 20s in the intensive care unit. He was battling morbid obesity, high blood pressure, and uncontrolled diabetes. Life felt heavy, and every step was a reminder of decline. Instead of lecturing, I told him: *"You don't need another pill, you need a warrior mentality. Every rep, every bite of food, every choice is either a fight or a fold."*

Something clicked. He started eating healthy and attacked the gym with a relentlessness that sweat alone could explain. Fast-forward: he's lost over 100 pounds, reversed his diabetes, and now runs triathlons and Spartan races. When he sent me a medal photo covered in mud, I laughed: *"I didn't mean that kind of Spartan but I'll take it!"*

This patient's story proves the prescription wasn't medicine; it was discipline. I feel so honored and blessed to ignite that spark. Failure didn't break this man; it became his blueprint for resilience.

Pivoting Through Pain

Hardship never ends. There will always be another storm, another betrayal, another loss. But resilience means you stop seeing these as tragedies and start seeing them as training. You can't always control what happens to you, but you're responsible for how you respond.

Pivoting is power. It's not about pretending you're unbreakable, it's about letting life break you, then coming back sharper. It's about losing, failing, bleeding, and still standing back up to say, *"Is that all you got?"* That's resilience. That's how you transform suffering into strength.

> *"Every day you're alive is a blessing. Life is too short to be weak."*
>
> — Adam Rajoulh, MD

Chapter 10

Money Moves - Financial Fitness

"Do not save what is left after spending, but spend what is left after saving."

— Warren Buffett

Money and Freedom

People love to say, "Money doesn't buy happiness." True. But let me be clear: not having money can make anyone miserable. Unless you're a single monk meditating somewhere in Tibet, most of us need money. We have families to feed, bills to pay, and futures to secure. Money buys autonomy. Freedom is everything. Nations have gone to war for it.

Story Time. Avoid My Mistakes

Here's a story that still makes me laugh, and cringe. When I first became an attending physician, I finally started making money after years of grinding through school and residency. And what did I do with that money? I leased a black, limited edition AMG C63 Mercedes-Benz convertible, a car so flashy it had to be shipped in from Arizona. My monthly payment? $1,850. At the time, I thought I'd made it. Rolling up to hospitals and with music blasting, chest out.

Reality checked me fast. One day, I pulled into the parking lot of a nursing home to meet the medical director, my boss at the site. He arrived in what appeared to be a beat-up 1996 Buick Regal. It looked like it came with a cassette GPS and dial up internet. Fred Flintstone wouldn't even drive it. He got out of his car, shook my hand, glanced at my car, smirked, and said:

"Nice car."

Later, I learned this man owned multiple nursing homes across California and was worth millions. Meanwhile, I was the young doctor in the convertible, trying to look rich while this dude quietly built empires. I felt like a fool. But I made sure to have the top down on my ride home.

That moment humbled me. It reminded me of a story about Jeff Bezos, when Amazon was already a multi-billion dollar company. A journalist asked him why he still drove an old Honda Accord. Bezos answered simply: "This is a perfectly good car." Warren Buffett also still drives a Cadillac. And Mark Zuckerberg dresses like Adam Sandler.

There's a reason the wealthy stay wealthy, it's not just because they make money, it's because they know what to do with it. Wealthy people don't stay wealthy by buying shiny objects. They understand what really matters: **assets over liabilities.**

Too many people, including athletes and entertainers, blow millions as quickly as they earn them. Making money isn't hard. Keeping it is the challenge. Growing it is the real test.

A Quick Disclaimer

I'm not a financial advisor and I'm not an accountant. I'm a physician. What I share here is based on my personal experience, not professional financial advice. I am not the Wolf of Wallstreet. However, most of my net worth has come from disciplined investing in the stock market. I don't day trade and I have no hidden course to sell. Actually wait for it... nope, still no course. My only goal is simple: I want you to succeed.

Be Careful Who You Listen To

Here's one rule I live by: **never take financial advice from someone who has less money than you.** Too many people brag about gross sales or flashy purchases while bleeding cash behind the scenes. A company that brings in $5 million but spends $6 million on marketing isn't successful, it's losing $1 million. Don't be fooled by smoke and mirrors. Always question the source. People be lyin'.

Assets vs. Liabilities

Robert Kiyosaki explained it best in *Rich Dad, Poor Dad*:

- Assets put money in your pocket.
- Liabilities take money out of your pocket.

It sounds simple, but most people get it wrong. A house you live in? Liability, unless it produces rental income. That flashy car? Liability. Investments, rental properties, index funds, dividend stocks? Assets.

The poor and middle class often collect liabilities that look like assets. They buy bigger houses, nicer cars, new gadgets, thinking they're building wealth. The rich quietly collect income-producing assets. Do I miss the way my baby used to purr for me every time I turned on the engine? The truth? No. I don't care about that crap anymore. My priorities shifted. I care about building a legacy. Assets over liabilities.

A Federal Reserve report found the top 10% of wealth holders in America had 65% of their net worth tied up in financial assets (stocks, bonds, business equity), while the bottom 50% had most of their wealth tied up in depreciating assets like cars and primary homes. That's not an accident, it's a mindset.

Modern Assets to Consider

- **Stocks & Index Funds** – The S&P 500 has averaged ~10% annual returns over the last century.
- **Tech & AI Stocks** – Microsoft, NVIDIA, Apple, Meta, Amazon are shaping the future.
- **Real Estate** – From rentals to REITs, tangible assets can generate cash flow.
- **Crypto** – High risk, high reward. Bitcoin and Ethereum now play a role in many diversified portfolios.
- **Businesses** – Starting your own or investing in others can create exponential returns.

Liabilities to Avoid

- Luxury cars (yes, my Mercedes)
- Credit card debt
- Over-mortgaged homes
- Lifestyle creep, spending more every time you earn more

Diversification Is Non-Negotiable

I believe in diversification. Never put all your eggs in one basket. Wealth isn't about one stream of income, it's about many. My portfolio spans stocks, bonds, property, and commodities. And right now, AI is my major focus. Diversification isn't optional, it's survival.

How Do You Actually Make Money?

People often ask, "Okay, but how do I start?" My advice: do something you know, something you're comfortable with, and something you're passionate about.

Growing up, I thought I'd be a WWE wrestler. Later, I thought I'd be a rapper. Then I grew up. Passion matters, but it has to intersect with skills and opportunity. For me, that was medicine. That's where my financial engine began.

The rule is simple: if it doesn't excite you and you're not obsessed with it, you won't stick with it. And if you won't stick with it, you won't thrive.

The Power of Passive Income

It's not just about working hard. It's about working smart. The ultimate goal is to get your money to work *for you*. That's why investing is so important, because it creates passive income.

Passive income means you're making money while you sleep. You're earning dividends while you're on vacation. Your assets are working even when you're not. And that kind of freedom is priceless.

Mitigate Your Risk

Whether in investing or in business, the goal isn't to avoid risk entirely, that's impossible. The goal is to minimize your risk by any means necessary.

Even when prescribing medicine to a patient, I always have to evaluate the risk/benefit ratio since some medicines for certain patients may result in more damage than benefit. Always know all the risks involved.

Study the risk, diversify, stay disciplined, and plan long term.

My Approach to Investing

I started investing later than I should have in my opinion but consistency changed everything.

My main financial rule: use logic over emotion. Money is not emotional. It's not a dinner date. I don't panic when stocks swing. I've never sold out of fear. The only people who get hurt on roller coasters are the ones who jump off too early. The stock market works the same way, patience pays.

Taxes: The Unsexy Essential

Taxes are one of the biggest silent wealth killers. If you don't understand them, you're handing extra money to Uncle Sam. In school, no one teaches you how to file taxes, set up an LLC, or manage business deductions, because the system is designed to prepare you to be an employee, not an owner. But if you want financial freedom, you have to learn this on your own.

The good news: when you pay attention, you keep more of what you earn. According to the IRS, taxpayers who itemized in 2021 reduced their taxable income by over **$1.3 trillion** combined. That's money that stayed in people's pockets instead of Washington's.

Whether through business write-offs, retirement contributions, or choosing the right structure for your income, taxes can either quietly drain your wealth or quietly protect it.

Some Data to Start Investing Now
- Financial stress is a leading cause of divorce and family breakdown (APA, 2018).
- Chronic debt increases risk of depression and anxiety disorders (Journal of Economic Psychology, 2019).
- Investors who start before age 30 are 7x more likely to retire millionaires compared to those who start after 40 (Vanguard, 2021).
- Index funds outperformed 85% of actively managed funds over the last 15 years (S&P SPIVA Report, 2022).

Compound Growth vs. Compound Debt

Debt compounds against you. Investments compound for you. Skip a few overpriced dinners, invest that money instead, and in 20 years you'll thank yourself.

- Credit cards → compound interest destroys you.
- Investments → compound growth builds you.

Albert Einstein called compound interest the "eighth wonder of the world." Whether he said it or not, the truth holds: compounding changes everything.

Lessons Learned
- Don't take financial advice from broke people.
- Delay gratification. That Mercedes gave me a dopamine hit; building wealth gave me peace.
- Diversify and have multiple sources of revenue, including passive income.
- Live below your means and invest the difference.
- Legacy > luxury. You can't take the money with you, but you can leave a blueprint for your family.

Money Moves Checklist
1. Eliminate high-interest debt (credit cards first).
2. Build assets, shrink liabilities.
3. Diversify across at least 3–5 asset classes (stocks, bonds, real estate, and commodities)
4. Automate monthly investments, even small ones, start investing early, even $100-200 per month matters.
5. Focus on passive income streams.
6. Avoid emotional decisions, money isn't a date night.
7. Remember: money = freedom.

The Discipline Link

Financial health isn't just math, it's mindset. The same mental muscle that keeps you grinding in the gym keeps you from blowing your paycheck on nonsense.
- Discipline in training → discipline in budgeting.
- Tracking your macros → tracking your expenses.

- Saying no to junk food → saying no to impulse buys.

Wealth, like muscle, isn't built overnight. It's the compound interest of small, consistent wins.

If you can't control a $5 Starbucks habit, don't expect to control a $500,000 mortgage.

Discipline is universal. Once you master it in one area whether it is fitness, food, finances, it bleeds into everything else.

The Duty to Build Wealth

This isn't just about you. It's about your family and generations after you. It's about leaving a legacy. Money isn't evil, it's a useful tool. And if God gave you the ability to make it, it's your duty to make it and use it wisely.

This chapter isn't financial theory. What I share here is real, lived experience. I've built wealth not through tricks, but through discipline and consistency, the same way I approach medicine, fitness, and life.

And the same way I want you to approach your future.

> *"Money may not buy happiness, but not having it will make you miserable."*
>
> —Adam Rajoulh, MD

Chapter 11

Digital Discipline: Rewiring Your Brain In The Age Of Distraction

"Technology is nothing. What's important is that you have faith in people, that they're basically good and smart, and if you give them tools, they'll do wonderful things with them."

— Steve Jobs

The Attention Crisis

I feel it is my responsibility to touch on *digital discipline* since we currently live in a digital era. We live in a world where the average person checks their phone **300 times a day.** Every ping, every ding, every scroll is engineered to hijack our focus.

And let's be honest, you probably checked your phone once between reading the last paragraph and this one. That's how powerful these devices are. They don't just sit in your pocket; they live rent free in your brain.

Your brain is like a muscle. Every time you resist distraction, you're doing a mental rep. Every time you give in, you reinforce weakness. If you feel more drained after 20 minutes of TikTok scrolling than after a 5K run, you're not imagining it; one is exercise, the other is a dopamine slot machine designed to keep you hooked.

The Dopamine Hijack

Here's the science: your brain runs on dopamine, the neurotransmitter of anticipation and reward. Every "like," notification, and autoplay video is a hit. But constant spikes desensitize your reward system. Soon, you need more stimulation just to feel the same baseline of satisfaction, leaving you restless, anxious, and unfocused.

Dr. Anna Lembke, author of *Dopamine Nation*, calls this the "pleasure-pain balance." Flood your brain with easy dopamine, and pain follows: boredom, irritability, craving. Balance is restored only by intentional discipline and strategic struggle. That's why exercise, fasting, or cold showers feel so grounding, they reset your dopamine baseline.

Translation? Your phone isn't just a tool. It's a portable dopamine syringe. Until you master it, it will master you.

Patient Story, Digital Attack

I once had a patient in his mid-40s who came in complaining of fatigue, anxiety, and "brain fog." He thought it was low testosterone. After labs, everything came back normal. The real culprit? His screen time report showed **12 hours a day** on his phone! He would literally spend half the day bouncing between emails, internet and social media. He was under what I call "digital attack!"

We built a simple plan: no phone 2 hours before bed, no social media before 10 a.m., and no phone during the gym (other than music) so he could train with purpose without any distractions. Within a month, his energy improved, his sleep stabilized, and his anxiety dropped more than any pill could have achieved. His "prescription" wasn't a supplement, it was *digital discipline.*

Screen Time and Mental Health

The research is clear: heavy screen time isn't just a distraction, it's linked to real mental health consequences.

- **Depression:** A large-scale study of U.S. adolescents found that teens who spent 5 or more hours per day on screens had double the risk of depression compared to those with 1 hour or less (Twenge et al., *J Abnorm Psychol*, 2019).
- **Anxiety:** A meta-analysis showed that problematic smart-phone use was strongly correlated with anxiety, stress, and poor sleep (Elhai et al., *Comput Human Behav*, 2017).
- **ADHD:** A prospective study of over 2,500 adolescents revealed that heavy use of digital media was associated with a two-fold increase in ADHD symptoms over two years (Ra et al., *JAMA*, 2018).

The bottom line? The more we live on screens, the more we risk rewiring our brains for restlessness, worry, and distraction. That's why **getting outside is medicine.**

Mother Nature is Healing

There's a reason you feel better after a walk outdoors, nature resets the nervous system in ways screens never will. One Stanford study found that a 90-minute walk in nature significantly reduced activity in the brain region linked to rumination and depression (Bratman et al., *PNAS*, 2015).

Sunlight also regulates circadian rhythms, boosting sleep quality and mood. In fact, sunlight exposure is one of the primary treatments for seasonal affective disorder (SAD), a type of depression triggered by reduced daylight during winter months (Melrose, *Neuropsychiatr Dis Treat*, 2015). Unlike the endless scroll, nature lowers cortisol, reduces anxiety, and improves attention span.

Even practices like grounding, which we looked at in chapter 6, remind us that the best antidote to tech overload is often as simple as stepping outside and reconnecting with nature.

Digital Minimalism

Digital discipline doesn't mean throwing your phone into the ocean and moving to a cabin (although some days that sounds tempting). It means using tech on *your* terms.

Practical strategies:
- **Notification Fasting** – Turn off everything that isn't essential.
- **Screen-Free Zones** – No phones in the bedroom. No phones at dinner. No phones 2 hours before bed.
- **Curate Your Inputs** – Junk food ruins your gut; junk information ruins your mind. Choose carefully.

- **Replace Don't Just Remove** – Don't just delete Instagram. Replace it with a book, a walk, journaling, or even real-life human conversation (yes, that still exists).

Mental stimulation (scrolling, news, TikTok drama) keeps your brain wired, even after you put the phone down. Blue light from screens suppresses melatonin (the hormone that helps you fall asleep) for at least 1-2 hours, hence the no phone 2 hours before bed.

If you need three alarms to get up because you're scrolling past the first two, it's not your phone that needs an update, it's your habits.

Or just get outside!

AI as a Tool, Not a Threat

AI is often painted as the villain, but when used correctly, it can be one of the greatest allies in health and performance.

- **Medicine:** Surgeons now use AI-assisted robotics (like the da Vinci Surgical System) to perform delicate operations with greater precision and fewer complications. AI algorithms are also being used to detect cancer on imaging scans earlier than human radiologists.
- **Cognitive Health:** AI-driven apps provide personalized brain-training for patients with Alzheimer's and dementia, improving memory and slowing decline.
- **Entrepreneurship & Daily Life:** AI can streamline scheduling, automate repetitive tasks, and even act as a thought partner, freeing mental bandwidth for higher level creativity and decision making.

The Mental Fitness Connection

Digital discipline isn't about restriction, it's about **sovereignty of attention.**

Mental fitness isn't just about resisting distraction, it's about **adaptation.**

And in today's world, adaptation means mastering your relationship with technology. We live in the age of AI, and that means the most "fit" minds will be the ones that learn how to harness it instead of fear it. It's our duty as humans to adapt and multiply our efficiency and impact. Those who resist will be left behind; those who adapt will thrive.

Action Step: The 7-Day Dopamine Detox

- **Day 1–2: Audit and Cut.** Track screen time; reduce by 20%.
- **Day 3–4: Social Media Fast.** 24 hours off. Notice the difference.
- **Day 5–6: Replace and Recharge.** Swap 30 minutes of scrolling for prayer, a walk, or journaling.
- **Day 7: Reflect and Lock In.** Pick one permanent habit to keep (ex: no phone in bed, or daily reading).

The Bottom Line

Technology isn't good or bad, it's neutral. It can steal your time or amplify your life. It can fragment your focus or fuel your purpose. The choice is yours.

> *"Technology can be the worst thing or the best thing, depending how you use it."*
>
> — Adam Rajoulh, MD

Chapter 12

Respect And Healthy Relationships

"The quality of your life is determined by the quality of your relationships."

— Tony Robbins

Relationships are the core of human experience. From family to friendships to professional networks, the way we connect defines much of our happiness, our opportunities, and even our health.

Science shows that social isolation is as dangerous to your health as smoking 15 cigarettes a day. That's not just clickbait, that's hard data.

Loneliness can increase your risk of premature death by 26% (Holt-Lunstad et al., 2015).

And on the flip side, the longest running study in history, Harvard's 80-year study on adult development, found one overwhelming truth: **the strength of your relationships is the single greatest predictor of happiness and longevity** (Harvard Study of Adult Development, 2017).

But relationships aren't just about avoiding loneliness. They're about building a foundation of respect. Respect for yourself. Respect for others. Respect for the boundaries that keep both sides healthy.

The Pillars of Healthy Relationships

Science and real life agree: strong relationships aren't accidents.

They're built. The most important pillars are simple:

- **Trust** – without it, nothing stands.
- **Respect** – the action that sustains love.
- **Communication** – say the hard things, don't let them rot in silence.
- **Boundaries** – respect them and enforce your own.
- **Shared values** – goals and principles aligned.
- **Support** – show up when it's inconvenient.
- **Humor** – if you can't laugh together, you'll cry apart.
- **Physical intimacy** – not just sex, but affection, presence, and connection.

The bottom line: love is the spark, but respect and effort are the fuel.

How to Win People

In *How to Win Friends and Influence People* (Dale Carnegie, 1936), the essential takeaway is that relationships flourish when grounded in appreciation, respect, and understanding. Carnegie argues that people crave recognition and they want to feel important. His strategies center around empathy, humility, and respect: don't criticize, condemn, or complain; give honest, sincere appreciation; and genuinely listen. These are not just niceties; they are the building blocks of trust and influence.

One memorable example Carnegie gives is of Charles M. Schwab, who rose to be paid a million dollars a year "largely because of his ability to handle people." Carnegie quotes Schwab saying: *"I consider my ability to arouse enthusiasm among my people the greatest asset I possess, and the way to develop the best that is in a person is by appreciation and encouragement."*

Because Schwab treated his employees with respect, encouraging them rather than chastising them, people wanted to go the extra mile.

Healthy vs Toxic Responses

Responding from a position of love and empathy rather than ego and defense is everything in *any* relationship.

Mistakes
- Healthy: *"We'll figure it out together."*
- Toxic: *"You always screw up."*

Stress
- Healthy: *"Rough day, can I vent?"*
- Toxic: *Silent treatment or blame.*

Success
- Healthy: *"I'm proud of you."*
- Toxic: *"Must be nice... I could have done that too."*

Disagreements
- Healthy: *"Let's talk this out, I want to understand."*
- Toxic: *Yelling, insults, or walking away.*

Boundaries

- Healthy: *"I respect that, you matter to me."*
- Toxic: *"That's stupid, why would you need that?"*

Reflection, Which replies does your relationship fall into more often? Be brutally honest.

Boundaries Build Respect

People often mistake boundaries for selfishness. Wrong. Boundaries are love in action. They tell the other person: *"Here's how we can make this relationship work."* Without boundaries, resentment festers. With boundaries, respect grows.

Saying "no" isn't cruelty, it's clarity. It's not about pushing people away, it's about protecting the relationship. Boundaries teach others how to treat you and show them that you take yourself seriously. When you respect your own time and energy, you invite others to do the same.

Think of it like the oxygen mask rule on an airplane, you put yours on first so you can actually help others. Boundaries work the same way. They aren't walls, they're guardrails. They keep your energy from being drained, your relationships from being poisoned by silent resentment, and your life from being pulled in every direction but your own. Setting limits doesn't weaken love, it strengthens it, because it's grounded in honesty and mutual respect.

Respect vs. Love

People get this wrong all the time: they put love on a pedestal. But love is an emotion, it comes and goes, just like fear or laughter. Respect, on the other hand, is an action. Respect is steady. Respect is earned. And respect sustains what love alone cannot.

Here's how I look at it: I love ice cream, but I don't respect it. You can "love" someone while still lying to them, betraying them, or taking them for granted. Without mutual respect, no relationship will last, whether it's with a colleague, a friend, a relative, or your life partner.

Coming from someone who's been divorced, I'll tell you straight: the two biggest lessons I've learned for couples are these:

1. Never go to bed upset.
2. Always respect each other.

Couples will always have conflicts. It's called life. However, when conflict arises, **your job is never to escalate, your job is to de- escalate**. Escalation is ego. De-escalation is respect. It's not about winning an argument; it's about preserving the bond.

I once had a patient who told me, "Doc, my wife and I fight like cats and dogs, but I've learned this: if one of us throws gas, the other one has to throw water." That stuck with me. Healthy relationships aren't about never arguing; they're about knowing how to keep the fire from burning the house down.

If you can hold on to those principles, you'll already be ahead of most people.

The Art of Fighting Fair

Every relationship, no matter how strong, will face conflict. The difference between couples or friendships that last and those that crumble is how they handle disagreements. Fighting fair means you attack the problem, not the person. It's about arguing like teammates, not enemies.

Here are a few principles of fighting fair:

- **Listen more than you talk.** Don't just wait for your turn to speak, actually try to understand the other person's point.
- **Don't keep score.** Bringing up every mistake from the past only poisons the present.
- **Use "I" statements.** "I feel hurt when..." is very different from "You always..."
- **Choose water, not gasoline.** In every argument, you have a choice, throw water to calm it down, or gasoline to blow it up.

Conflict is inevitable, but destruction is optional. When you learn the art of fighting fair, your relationships grow stronger through challenges instead of breaking under them.

Leadership and Toxic Masculinity

If you look at society nowadays, you'll notice a strange role reversal. More women are stepping into traditionally male roles, while more men are stepping into traditionally female ones. Let's be real gentlemen. We need to assume personal responsibility - **we did this to ourselves.**

Our society has become weak. Men are walking around with nail polish and fanny packs and taking selfies with foam art. I remember when men used to hunt with their bare hands and now they're in line waiting for matcha.

Here's the thing, I don't care if you like matcha. I don't even care if you want to wear skinny jeans so tight they cut off circulation to your future kids. But what I do care about is when men abandon their roles as protectors, providers, and leaders.

Masculinity doesn't mean domination. It means protection. It means provision. It means discipline. It means being the steady rock when life throws storms. That's not oppression; that's purpose. In relationships, respect is leadership.

Let me be clear: it's not "toxic masculinity" for a man to lead. Leading is not domination, that's responsibility. Leadership isn't toxic. Strength isn't toxic. Responsibility isn't toxic. What's toxic is apathy. What's toxic is weakness disguised as "acceptance."

Providing for your family, protecting them, and nurturing them is not "extra credit." It's the bare minimum. Decades ago, this was expected. Now, it's treated like a luxury. We live in an era of entitlement, where people think they deserve the world without putting in the work. But true respect, like true leadership, is earned through action, not demanded by words.

And here's the thing: leadership in relationships isn't about control, it's about example. Your kids will watch how you treat their mother. Your partner will watch how you handle pressure. Respect isn't taught by lectures; it's modeled by behavior. When a father shows respect in his actions, he teaches his son how to be a man and his daughter what to expect from one. That's leadership.

Your Network Is Your Net Worth

Your circle matters. Your environment matters. It's true about your network being your net worth. If you surround yourself with people who drain you, pull you down, or poison you with negativity, don't be surprised when you feel stuck.

"You are the average of the five people you spend the most time with." You've heard it before, but have you lived it? If you want to be disciplined, motivated, and positive, you can't surround yourself with lazy, toxic people. It's like trying to eat clean while living inside a Krispy Kreme.

This doesn't mean you cut out everyone who isn't perfect. It means you're intentional. Choose relationships that fuel you, not ones that drain you. Cut out the energy suckers. Limit your time with people of low vibration. Choose people with similar values and goals. Surround yourself with people who challenge you, support you, and want you to win.

The Power of Community

Humans weren't designed to thrive alone. From an evolutionary standpoint, survival meant belonging to a tribe, isolation often meant death. Our ancestors hunted, protected, and raised families together. That same biology still runs through us today, which is why loneliness can be so destructive. Research shows that strong social bonds significantly improve physical health, mental well- being, and even longevity (Holt-Lunstad et al., 2015)

But community isn't just about survival, it's about becoming your best self. Surrounding yourself with people who push, mentor, and support you changes the trajectory of your life. I am blessed to have my family and lifelong brothers. You know who you are.

A good mentor can compress decades of wisdom into days, saving you from mistakes and accelerating your growth. Think of it as building your own "tribe": a circle of accountability partners who challenge your excuses, mentors who expand your vision, and opportunities to serve others.

Community sharpens you, grounds you, and lifts you when your own strength isn't enough.

Action Step: Write down three people who could form the foundation of your "tribe." Choose one person to be your accountability partner, one person you'd like as a mentor, and one person you can serve. Reach out to each this week, even a single text can start building your tribe.

Respect Is Legacy

At the end of the day, your relationships define your legacy. Not your car, not your bank account, not your resume. People won't remember your salary; they'll remember how you made them feel.

Strong relationships are built on respect, not entitlement. On effort, not convenience. On showing up, not checking out.

The ultimate respect is serving others. Respect isn't passive, it's active. It's checking in on a friend when you don't have to. It's forgiving when it's hard. It's choosing patience instead of anger. Respect is legacy in motion.

Empathy is Essential

Empathy is the ability to *feel with* someone, not just *feel for* them. It's stepping into their shoes, seeing the world through their eyes, and understanding their emotions, even if you don't agree with them.

Empathy is not just a feeling, it's biological. "Mirror neurons" in the brain activate when we see someone else in pain, lighting up the same regions as if we were experiencing it ourselves. Empathy doesn't make you weak, it makes you human, and the toughest people I know are also the most empathetic because they understand pain and refuse to pass it on. Think about that.

The second you start keeping score in relationships, you've already poisoned them, do good because it's who you are, not because you're waiting for applause. Have empathy, be honest in your encounters with good intentions, and don't expect things in return. I've already instilled this with my six year old daughter.

Energy is real: walk into a room and you can instantly feel who's bitter, who's fake, and who's thriving, and people will always remember how you made them feel long after they forget your words.

Remember, karma is undefeated. You might outrun it for a while, but sooner or later the bill comes due. Plant poison, reap poison. Plant generosity, reap blessings. That's the law.

Build relationships that make you better. Be the kind of person who raises the bar for everyone around you. And when people speak your name after you're gone, let them remember how you improved their life.

> *"Love is a feeling. Respect is an action. Respect is the real currency."*

— Adam Rajoulh, MD

Chapter 13

Serving Others - A Legacy Of Purpose

"The best way to find yourself is to lose yourself in the service of others."

— Mahatma Gandhi

Creating Legacy

At some point, life has to become bigger than you. Most of us live in a cycle of me, me, me, my bills, my stress, my body, my goals. But real legacy begins when your vision expands past your own reflection.

For me, that shift began during the happiest day of my life, when I delivered my daughter, Leena, with my own hands. That priceless beautiful moment reminded me that purpose isn't just about achievement, it's about building something that outlives you. Something she and her children can point to and say, *"This is what my father stood for."*

Legacy isn't just wealth. It isn't just buildings, businesses, or financial accounts. Those fade. Legacy is reputation. Legacy is service. It's what people remember when your name is spoken years after you're gone. When you're no longer on this earth, how do YOU want to be remembered?

I know that when I die, I don't want to be remembered just for working hard. I want my bloodline to remember me as a man who helped others before helping himself. A man who fed others before feeding himself. A man who stood for truth at all costs. A man who used his strength, knowledge, and blessings not to hoard, but to serve humanity.

Harnessing Spiritual Strength

Spiritual strength isn't a sexy topic that is trending on TikTok. It's overlooked, ignored, and yet it's the backbone of everything. Someone who is strong spiritually cannot be broken, period.

Spiritual strength is your ability to stay grounded, resilient, and purposeful in the face of hardship, anchored not just by your emotions or logic, but by a deeper set of values, beliefs, or connection to something bigger than yourself.

And this is not to be confused with someone who is religious. Someone can regularly partake in religious ceremonies out of routine and still be spiritually weak. Somebody can pray daily while also committing atrocious sins, refusing to learn and evolve from their mistakes. Spiritual strength refers to:

- **Clarity of values:** Knowing what you stand for, so when life shakes you, you don't crumble.
- **Inner resilience:** Staying calm and unshaken even when everything external is chaos.
- **Purpose beyond self:** Living for more than comfort or pleasure, but for service, love, or legacy.
- **Acceptance of imperfection:** Recognizing that pain, failure, and loss are part of life, and finding meaning in them.

- **Connection to higher meaning:** Whether through God, faith, nature, philosophy, or your own code of ethics.

Think of it like this: *mental strength gets you through tough days, but spiritual strength gets you through the storms that don't end.*

A great example of true spiritual strength is my father. Literally nothing breaks him. We could be having a zombie apocalypse while the sky rains fireballs, and he would still be calm, unfazed, and immovable. I've always admired this about him the most. It literally shaped his unbreakable being.

And don't worry, Mom, I won't forget to mention you. You're a selfless angel who would sacrifice everything for your children, and your momma's boy loves you the most.

Doing Good vs. Feeling Good

If your priority is to feel good, you'll be miserable. You'll chase highs like a junkie, likes, purchases, applause, dopamine hits. It's a treadmill you can't get off. The more you feed it, the hungrier it gets, and the emptier you feel when the buzz wears off. Feeling good is temporary, and if you make it the end goal, you'll always be at the mercy of circumstance and other people's validation.

But if your priority is doing good, you flip the script. Purpose doesn't fade when the applause dies. Doing good anchors you. When you're focused on serving, building, giving, or creating something bigger than yourself, you'll find that fulfillment outlasts the dopamine rush. That's where legacy comes from, not in what you felt, but in what you built.

No matter how big your problems are, your purpose will always be bigger. Always remember your purpose, your "why." Pain shrinks and eventually fades when it's stacked up against meaning and purpose. And here's the irony: when you stop chasing "feeling good" and start living to *do* good, the deep, lasting kind of good feelings sneak in on their own, peace, pride, gratitude. That's the kind of high that never crashes.

Owning Your Values

Most of the time, when we feel overwhelmed, it isn't because of our own values being out of alignment, it's because we're measuring ourselves by somebody else's yardstick.

The first step is asking: *Am I chasing goals that are actually mine, or goals that society told me to want?*

For me, my compass is clear: be a good father, a good son, a good doctor, and a good man, and leave behind a positive legacy attached to my name.

That doesn't mean I never slip. I've failed more times than I can count. But I return to purpose again and again.

The Whisper of Weakness

We are all imperfect. And imperfection doesn't disqualify you from greatness. Kanye West once rapped in *Jesus Walks*: "I want to talk to God, but I'm afraid 'cause we ain't spoke in so long." That line captures how guilt works. You can commit sins or stop praying and think it's too late for God to listen to you since you turned your back.

That's the lie the devil whispers in your ear, to keep you weak, to keep you ashamed, and to keep you living without purpose. Don't believe that lie. Imperfection does not disqualify you from greatness. Falling short doesn't end the story. Quitting does.

Imperfection Is Not Failure

Legacy is built in the small, imperfect steps forward. It's a compounding effect. It's built in showing up when you don't feel like it, in forgiving yourself when you fall short, and in returning to your purpose again and again.

Not following your goals 100% is okay. Using imperfection as an excuse to quit is not. I admire people like Kobe Bryant who were obsessive about their goals. But here's the truth: I'm not Kobe, and neither are you. And that's okay.

I don't always hit my *Power Protocol* every day. Life is messy. I'm a father, a physician, and a man juggling real responsibilities. Perfection isn't practical.

Missing a habit once is not the problem; missing twice is. Consistency matters more than intensity. *Focus on trajectory, not perfection.*

Building a Legacy Through Service

Service transforms strength into legacy. True warriors fight not for themselves but for others. Mother Teresa devoted her life to serving the poorest of the poor in Calcutta, proving that greatness is measured not by what you achieve, but by how much you give.

Action Step: Choose one act of service this week, mentor a colleague, volunteer your time, or simply listen deeply to someone who needs it. Strength grows when you lift others.

Serving others is about refusing to quit, refusing to let excuses run your life, and modeling resilience for the people who will carry your name long after you're gone.

Your kids don't need you to be flawless, they need you to be consistent. Your community doesn't need you to be rich, they need you to be reliable.

That's the final truth: once you've built yourself, your duty is to build others. Once you've been blessed, your job is to bless others. If God gave you strength, you're meant to pay that strength forward. That's how you create a legacy of purpose. This is how we evolve as mankind, not through selfish gain, but through universal gain.

> *"You may die one day, but your purpose and legacy shall live on."*

— Adam Rajoulh, MD

Mental Fitness

30 Day Challenge

Go ahead and pat yourself on the back for finishing this book. You have already taken an active step to improve your life and you should be proud! However, knowledge without execution is just trivia.

This is where you stop reading and start doing.

This isn't a magic formula. It's not 30 days to six-pack abs or 30 days to perfect happiness. It's 30 days to build momentum, to prove to yourself that you can actually live *Mental Fitness*, not just highlight it.

Week 1: Master the Basics (Sleep + Gratitude)

- Lock in 7–9 hours of sleep. Non-negotiable.
- Cut caffeine after 2 PM.
- Write down 3 things you're grateful for every morning.
- No phone for the first 10 minutes of your day.

Why? Because this resets your body and your perspective. Everything else builds on this.

Week 2: Build the Body (Movement + Nutrition)

- Move every day (lift, run, walk, fight, stretch, I don't care, just move).

- Eat real food. Cut the crap with 20 ingredients on the label.
- Protein with every meal (no, not just because I'm a "meathead doctor," but because the science says muscle equals longevity).
- One cold shower or sauna session this week to test your discomfort muscle.

Week 3: Train the Mind (Mental Fitness Drills)
- 10 minutes daily of silence: meditation, prayer, or breath work.
- Visualize your future self like an architect with a blueprint. Then take one small action toward it.
- No complaining challenge: go 24 hours without a single complaint. If you slip, restart the clock.
- Read or listen to something that challenges your brain every day.

Week 4: Purpose + Service (The Legacy Step)
- Do one act of service every day, big or small. Hold the door. Call your mom. Mentor someone.
- Journal: "What legacy do I want to leave behind?" Write freely for 10 minutes.
- Share your journey with someone. Inspire them to start.
- End the week by writing a note to your future self, sealing your commitment.

Day 30: The Line in the Sand
On the final day, write down two things:
1. The biggest change you felt over these 30 days.
2. The biggest excuse you killed.

Then sign it. Date it. That's your contract.

The Rule of Compounding

None of these tasks are overwhelming on their own. But compounded over 30 days, they will transform your mind, your body, and your purpose. The compounding effect doesn't just build habits, it builds identity.

At the end of 30 days, you won't just have completed a challenge. You'll have redefined what's possible.

Journaling Prompts for Mental Fitness

Reflection turns knowledge into wisdom. Each night, take five minutes to jot down:

- What did I do today that strengthened my health, power, or purpose?
- Where did I slip, and what can I adjust tomorrow?
- What's one thing I'm grateful for today?

These prompts are simple, but they train your brain to track progress and reframe setbacks as opportunities.

Weekly Checkpoints

Week 1: Focus on consistency, hit your nutrition, fitness, or sleep goal at least 80% of the time.

Week 2: Add a relationship or community goal, reach out to one person you respect or admire.

Week 3: Audit your digital life, cut out at least one habit that wastes time or energy.

Week 4: Reflect on growth, write down three things you can carry forward into the next 30 days.

Mental Fitness Daily Protocol

Your Daily Checklist for *Health, Power, and Purpose*

Move your body, at least 30 minutes of strength, cardio, or even a walk. Motion creates momentum.

Fuel smart, prioritize protein, whole foods, and hydration. Cut the processed junk.

Sleep like it matters, aim for 7–9 hours; shut off screens 1-2 hours before bed.

Stress reset, practice breathwork, journaling, or meditation for 5–10 minutes.

Gratitude practice, write down three things you're grateful for every morning or night.

Build your tribe, connect with someone you respect, learn from, or uplift daily.

Digital discipline, limit screen time; use technology for creation, not just consumption.

Purpose check, ask yourself: "Did I move closer to my mission today?" If not, reset tomorrow.

Now imagine this: You start the challenge exhausted, distracted, and unsure. By Week 2, you notice your sleep improving and your energy rising. By Week 3, you're less glued to your phone and more present with people you love. By the end of the month, you've built small wins into systems. You don't just feel fitter, you feel in control.

This is the point: thirty days isn't about perfection. It's about **proving to yourself that change is possible**, then using that momentum to keep going.

Remember, life is your biggest blessing. And wasting it is the biggest tragedy.

REFERENCES NOTE

Mental Fitness is supported by roughly 100 scientific references drawn from leading journals, institutions, and landmark studies in psychology, neuroscience, nutrition, and medicine. They are provided here for readers who want to explore further or dive deeper into the science.

While this book is written to be practical and accessible, every principle and recommendation is grounded in evidence.

REFERENCES

Algoe, S. B. *Find, remind, and bind: The functions of gratitude in everyday relationships. Social and Personality Psychology Compass*, 2012.

American Heart Association. *Poor sleep and cardiovascular disease risk.* 2020. https://www.heart.org

American Psychological Association. *Stress in America: The state of our nation.* 2018.

https://www.apa.org/news/press/releases/stress/2018/state-nation

American Psychological Association. *Resilience and stress management.*

2022. https://www.apa.org/topics/resilience

Anderson, J. W., & Nunnelley, P. A. *Private prayer associations with depression, anxiety, and health outcomes: A systematic review. Alternative Therapies in Health and Medicine*, 2019.

Basaria, S., Coviello, A. D., Travison, T. G., et al. *Adverse events associated with testosterone administration. New England Journal of Medicine*, 2010.

Belenky, G., et al. *Patterns of performance degradation and restoration during sleep restriction and recovery. Sleep*, 2003.

Bonanno, G. A. *Loss, trauma, and human resilience. American Psychologist*, 2004.

Booth, F. W., Roberts, C. K., & Laye, M. J. *Lack of exercise is a major cause of chronic diseases. Comprehensive Physiology*, 2012.

Bratman, G. N., et al. *Nature experience reduces rumination and subgenual prefrontal cortex activation. PNAS*, 2015.

Cappuccio, F. P., et al. *Sleep duration predicts cardiovascular outcomes: A systematic review and meta-analysis. European Heart Journal*, 2011.

Carnegie, D. *How to Win Friends and Influence People.* Simon & Schuster, 1936.

Centers for Disease Control and Prevention. *Insufficient sleep is a public health problem.* 2016. https://www.cdc.gov/sleep

Centers for Disease Control and Prevention. *Nutrition, physical activity, and obesity: Data and statistics.* 2019. https://www.cdc.gov/nccdphp

Centers for Disease Control and Prevention. *Sleep and sleep disorders.* 2022. https://www.cdc.gov/sleep

Centers for Disease Control and Prevention. *Chronic disease risk factors.*

2022. https://www.cdc.gov/chronicdisease

Centers for Disease Control and Prevention. *Physical activity and health.*

2023. https://www.cdc.gov/physicalactivity

Cespedes Feliciano, E. M., et al. *Sleep duration, restfulness, and mortality in the Women's Health Initiative. Sleep Health*, 2018.

Chevalier, G., Sinatra, S. T., Oschman, J. L., & Delany, R. M. *Earthing:*

Health implications of reconnecting the human body to the Earth's surface electrons. *Journal of Inflammation Research*, 2015.

Childs, E., & de Wit, H. *Regular exercise and emotional resilience to acute stress in healthy adults. Psychopharmacology*, 2014.

Cialdini, R. B. *Influence: The Psychology of Persuasion.* Harper Business, 2006.

Crum, A. J., Salovey, P., & Achor, S. *Rethinking stress: The role of mindsets in determining the stress response. Journal of Personality and Social Psychology*, 2013.

Cryan, J. F., & Dinan, T. G. *Mind-altering microorganisms: The impact of the gut microbiota on brain and behaviour. Nature Reviews Neuroscience*, 2012.

Czeisler, C. A., & Gooley, J. J. *Sleep and circadian rhythms in humans. Cold Spring Harbor Symposia on Quantitative Biology*, 2007.

De Souza, R. J., et al. *Intake of saturated and trans fats and risk of mortality, cardiovascular disease, and type 2 diabetes. BMJ*, 2015.

Duckworth, A. L., Peterson, C., Matthews, M. D., & Kelly, D. R. *Grit: Perseverance and passion for long-term goals. Journal of Personality and Social Psychology*, 2007.

Elhai, J. D., Dvorak, R. D., Levine, J. C., & Hall, B. J. *Problematic smartphone use: A conceptual overview and systematic review. Computers in Human Behavior*, 2017.

Emmons, R. A., & McCullough, M. E. *Counting blessings versus burdens:*

Gratitude and well-being. Journal of Personality and Social Psychology, 2003.

Emmons, R. A., & McCullough, M. E. *The Psychology of Gratitude.* Oxford University Press, 2004.

Epel, E. S., et al. *Accelerated telomere shortening in response to life stress. PNAS*, 2004.

Esteva, A., et al. *Dermatologist-level classification of skin cancer with deep neural networks. Nature*, 2017.

Fox, G. R., Kaplan, J., Damasio, H., & Damasio, A. *Neural correlates of gratitude. Social Cognitive and Affective Neuroscience*, 2015.

Froh, J. J., Sefick, W. J., & Emmons, R. A. *Counting blessings in early adolescents: An experimental study. Journal of School Psychology*, 2008.

Froh, J. J., Yurkewicz, C., & Kashdan, T. B. *Gratitude and well-being in early adolescence: Gender differences. Journal of Adolescence*, 2009.

GAO. *Workplace wellness programs: Better guidance needed.* U.S. Government Accountability Office, 2019.

Ghaly, M., & Teplitz, D. *The biological effects of grounding during sleep: Cortisol levels and stress. Journal of Alternative and Complementary Medicine*, 2004.

Gottman, J. M., & Silver, N. *The Seven Principles for Making Marriage Work.* Harmony Books, 2015.

Hall, K. D., et al. *Ultra-processed diets cause excess calorie intake and weight gain. Cell Metabolism*, 2019.

Haanel, C. F. *The Master Key System.* Psychiana Press, 1912.

Harvard Study of Adult Development. *Eighty-year longitudinal research on happiness and health.* Harvard Medical School, 2017.

Hewlings, S. J., & Kalman, D. S. *Curcumin: A review of its effects on human health. Foods*, 2017.

Holt-Lunstad, J., Smith, T. B., Baker, M., Harris, T., & Stephenson, D. *Loneliness and social isolation as risk factors for mortality: A meta-analytic review. Perspectives on Psychological Science*, 2015.

Hu, F. B. *Dietary pattern analysis: A new direction in nutritional epidemiology. Current Opinion in Lipidology*, 2002.

IRS. *Statistics of income reports.* Internal Revenue Service, 2021. https://www.irs.gov

Irwin, M., et al. *Partial night sleep deprivation reduces natural killer and immune responses. Psychosomatic Medicine*, 1994.

JAMA Psychiatry. *Association of ultra-processed food consumption with risk of depression. JAMA Psychiatry*, 2023.

Jeffers, S. *Feel the Fear and Do It Anyway.* Ballantine Books, 1987.

Kini, P., Wong, J., McInnis, S., Gabana, N., & Brown, J. W. *The effects of gratitude expression on neural activity. Frontiers in Psychology*, 2016.

Kiyosaki, R. T. *Rich Dad Poor Dad.* Warner Business Books, 1997.

Kraemer, W. J., & Ratamess, N. A. *Fundamentals of resistance training: Progression and exercise prescription. Medicine & Science in Sports & Exercise*, 2004.

Lally, P., van Jaarsveld, C. H., Potts, H. W., & Wardle, J. *How are habits formed: Modelling habit formation in the real world. European Journal of Social Psychology*, 2009.

Landi, F., Calvani, R., Tosato, M., et al. *Sarcopenia and mortality risk in frail older persons. Clinical Nutrition*, 2012.

Laukkanen, T., et al. *Association Between Sauna Bathing and Mortality. JAMA Internal Medicine*, 2015. Lembke, A. *Dopamine Nation*. Dutton, 2021.

Li, Q., Morimoto, K., Kobayashi, M., et al. *Visiting a forest increases natural killer activity and expression of anti-cancer proteins. International Journal of Immunopathology and Pharmacology*, 2008.

Longo, V. D., & Mattson, M. P. *Fasting: Molecular Mechanisms and Clinical Applications. Cell Metabolism*, 2014.

MacDougall, J. D., Sale, D. G., Moroz, D. E., Elder, G. C., Sutton, J. R., & Howald, H. *Mitochondrial volume density in human skeletal muscle after heavy resistance training. Medicine & Science in Sports & Exercise*, 1979.

Mattson, M. P., Longo, V. D., & Harvie, M. *Impact of intermittent fasting on health and disease processes. Ageing Research Reviews*, 2017.

McAuley, E., Blissmer, B., Marquez, D. X., Jerome, G. J., Kramer, A. F., & Katula, J. *Social relations, physical activity, and well-being in older adults. Preventive Medicine*, 2000.

McCraty, R., Atkinson, M., Tomasino, D., & Bradley, R. T. *The Coherent Heart*. HeartMath Institute, 2009.

McCraty, R., Atkinson, M., Rein, G., & Watkins, A. D. *Music enhances positive emotional states on salivary IgA. Stress Medicine*, 1998.

McEwen, B. S. *Physiology and neurobiology of stress and adaptation: Central role of the brain. Nature Neuroscience*, 2007.

Meeusen, R., Duclos, M., Foster, C., et al. *Endorphins and exercise: Physiological mechanisms and clinical implications. Sports Medicine,* 2011.

Melrose, S. *Seasonal Affective Disorder: Overview of assessment and treatment. Neuropsychiatric Disease and Treatment,* 2015.

Mills, P. J., Redwine, L., Wilson, K., Pung, M. A., Chinh, K., Greenberg, B. H., & Maisel, A. *The role of gratitude in spiritual well- being in asymptomatic heart failure patients. Spirituality in Clinical Practice,* 2015.

National Heart, Lung, and Blood Institute. *Poor sleep and cardiovascular disease risk.* 2020. https://www.nhlbi.nih.gov

National Institute on Aging. *What happens to the brain during sleep.* 2020.

https://www.nia.nih.gov

National Institutes of Health. *Sleep, obesity, and diabetes.* 2019.

https://www.nih.gov

Newport, C. *Digital Minimalism.* Penguin, 2019.

NIH. *Mind-body practices and health.* National Institutes of Health, 2021. https://www.nih.gov

NIMH. *Depression: Overview.* National Institute of Mental Health, 2022. https://www.nimh.nih.gov

NINDS. *Stroke: Hope through research.* National Institute of Neurological

Disorders and Stroke, 2021. https://www.ninds.nih.gov

ODPHP. *Physical Activity Guidelines for Americans, 2nd ed.* Office of Disease

Prevention and Health Promotion, 2018. https://health.gov

Park, B. J., Tsunetsugu, Y., Kasetani, T., et al. *Physiological effects of forest bathing in humans. Environmental Health and Preventive Medicine*, 2010.

Parr, E. B., Camera, D. M., Areta, J. L., et al. *Alcohol ingestion impairs post-exercise muscle protein synthesis. PLoS One*, 2014.

Pascual-Leone, A., Amedi, A., Fregni, F., & Merabet, L. B. *The plastic human brain cortex. Annual Review of Neuroscience*, 2005.

Patterson, R. E., & Sears, D. D. *Metabolic Effects of Intermittent Fasting. Annual Review of Nutrition*, 2017.

Przybylski, A. K., & Weinstein, N. *Digital screen time limits and mental well-being in adolescents. Nature Human Behaviour*, 2017.

Ra, C. K., Cho, J., Stone, M. D., et al. *Digital media use and symptoms of ADHD among adolescents. JAMA*, 2018.

Robert, P., et al. *Computer-based cognitive stimulation for Alzheimer's disease:*

A randomized clinical trial. Alzheimer's & Dementia, 2014.

Soon, C. S., Brass, M., Heinze, H. J., & Haynes, J. D. *Unconscious determinants of free decisions in the human brain. Nature Neuroscience*, 2008.

S&P Dow Jones Indices. *SPIVA U.S. Scorecard.* 2022.

https://www.spglobal.com/spdji

Sansone, R. A., & Sansone, L. A. *Gratitude and well-being: The benefits of appreciation.* Psychiatry (Edgmont), 2010.

SEC. *Investor education resources.* U.S. Securities and Exchange Commission, 2020. https://www.sec.gov

Seligman, M. E. P. *Flourish: A Visionary New Understanding of Happiness and Well-Being.* Free Press, 2011.

Song, D. K., et al. *Intermittent Fasting: Narrative Review.* Diabetes & Metabolism Journal, 2022.

Srikanthan, P., & Karlamangla, A. S. *Muscle mass index as a predictor of longevity.* American Journal of Medicine, 2014.

Stanley, T. J., & Danko, W. D. *The Millionaire Next Door.* 1996.

Ströhle, A. *Physical activity, exercise, depression, and anxiety disorders.* Journal of Neural Transmission, 2009.

Tedeschi, R. G., & Calhoun, L. G. *Posttraumatic growth: Conceptual foundations and empirical evidence.* Psychological Inquiry, 2004.

Twenge, J. M., & Campbell, W. K. *Associations between screen time and lower psychological well-being among children and adolescents.* Journal of Abnormal Psychology, 2019.

U.S. Census Bureau. *Health insurance coverage in the United States.* 2020.

https://www.census.gov

USDA & HHS. *Dietary Guidelines for Americans, 2020–2025.* 2020.

https://www.dietaryguidelines.gov

U.S. Department of Health and Human Services. *Physical Activity*

Guidelines for Americans, 2nd ed. 2020. https://health.gov

U.S. Government Accountability Office. *Workplace wellness programs: Better guidance needed.* 2019. https://www.gao.gov

U.S. Internal Revenue Service. *Statistics of income reports.* 2021. https://www.irs.gov

U.S. Securities and Exchange Commission. *Investor education resources.* 2020. https://www.sec.gov

Van Dongen, H. P. A., Maislin, G., Mullington, J. M., & Dinges, D. F. *The cumulative cost of additional wakefulness: Dose–response effects on neurobehavioral functions. Sleep*, 2003.

Vanguard. *Principles for Investing Success.* Vanguard Research, 2021.

Waldinger, R., & Schulz, M. S. *The Harvard Study of Adult Development: Lessons from an 80-year study of happiness.* Harvard Medical School / TED Talk, 2017.

Walker, M. P. *Why We Sleep: Unlocking the Power of Sleep and Dreams.* Scribner, 2017.

Wen, C. P., Wai, J. P., Tsai, M. K., et al. *Minimum amount of physical activity for reduced mortality and extended life expectancy. The Lancet*, 2011.

World Health Organization. *Physical activity fact sheet.* 2020. https://www.who.int

World Health Organization. *Guidelines on physical activity and sedentary behaviour.* 2021. https://www.who.int

World Health Organization. *World Mental Health Report: Transforming mental health for all.* 2022. https://www.who.int

World Health Organization. *Obesity and overweight fact sheet.* 2023. https://www.who.int

Wolfe, R. R. *Muscle's underappreciated role in health and disease.* American Journal of Clinical Nutrition, 2006.

Wood, A. M., Froh, J. J., & Geraghty, A. W. *Gratitude and well-being: A review and theoretical integration.* Clinical Psychology Review, 2010.

Zaccaro, A., et al. *How breath-control can change your life: A systematic review on psycho-physiological correlates of slow breathing.* Frontiers in Human Neuroscience, 2018.

About The Author

Adam Rajoulh, MD is a board-certified hospitalist physician, entrepreneur, *mental fitness* coach and trusted medical voice.

But titles don't tell the whole story. What defines him isn't just medicine, it's the battles outside of it. He's dealt with loss.

He's been broke. He's been beaten physically and mentally. He's been divorced, arrested, and defamed. Each setback became a forge. Each failure became fuel. As a physician, he's treated thousands of patients on the front lines of medicine, witnessing the same patterns repeat themselves: those who thrive take ownership and those who suffer fall into victimhood.

Mental Fitness isn't just another health book, it's a blueprint to confront pain, eliminate excuses, overcome failure, and leave a purposeful legacy. This book is more than advice, it's a manifesto. An accumulation of Dr. Rajoulh's wins and losses, his failures and comebacks, and his years of medical knowledge distilled into principles anyone can apply.

Through this work, Dr. Rajoulh's mission is clear: to help millions achieve health, power, and purpose. His promise is simple: every reader will walk away with something that will improve their life.

Raw. Scientific. Authentic. That's *Mental Fitness*, a contribution to a world that desperately needs strength over excuses.

My Final Words

Thank you for having the courage to read this book. Thank you for refusing to settle for mediocrity. Thank you for betting on yourself.

Be proud. You've already proven you're serious about change. Most people never make it this far. You did.

Now it's on you. Don't let this book collect dust. Live it. Put it into practice. Be the one in your family who breaks the cycle. Be the one who turns pain into power, and power into purpose.

If this book made you think, laugh, or see life a little differently, please take a minute to leave a quick review on Amazon.

Your feedback helps others discover *Mental Fitness* and supports my mission to help people live with more health, power, and purpose.

—Adam Rajoulh, MD

www.ingramcontent.com/pod-product-compliance
Lightning Source LLC
LaVergne TN
LVHW020933090426
835512LV00020B/3336